Spanish Teacher's BOOK OF INSTANT WORD GAMES

Over 160 Ready-to-Use Activities, Puzzles, and Worksheets for Grades 7-12

Josephine Carreño

THE CENTER FOR APPLIED RESEARCH IN EDUCATION
West Nyack, New York 10994

Library of Congress Cataloging-in-Publication Data

Carreño. Josephine.
    Spanish teacher's book of instant word games / Josephine Carreño.
      p. cm.
    ISBN 0-87628-757-7 (s). — ISBN 0-87628-892-1 (p)
    1. Spanish language—Study and teaching—English speakers.
  2. Educational games.   I. Title.
    PC4129.E5C36 1996
    468'.007—dc20

96-20549
CIP

Printed in the United States of America

10 9 8 7 6 5 4 3 2 1

ISBN 0-87628-757-7(s)   ISBN 0-87628-892-1(p)

Illustrations

by Josephine Carreño

ATTENTION: CORPORATIONS AND SCHOOLS

The Center for Applied Research in Education books are available at quantity discounts with bulk purchase for educational, business, or sales promotional use. For information, please write to: Prentice Hall Career & Personal Development Special Sales, 113 Sylvan Avenue, Englewood Cliffs, NJ 07632. Please supply: title of book, ISBN number, quantity, how the book will be used, date needed.

**THE CENTER FOR APPLIED RESEARCH
IN EDUCATION**
West Nyack, NY 10994
A Simon & Schuster Company

On the World Wide Web at http://www.phdirect.com

Prentice Hall International (UK) Limited, *London*
Prentice Hall of Australia Pty. Limited, *Sydney*
Prentice Hall Canada, Inc., *Toronto*
Prentice Hall Hispanoamericana, S.A., *Mexico*
Prentice Hall of India Private Limited, *New Delhi*
Prentice Hall of Japan, Inc., *Tokyo*
Simon & Schuster Asia Pte. Ltd., *Singapore*
Editora Prentice Hall do Brasil, Ltds., *Rio de Janeiro*

DEDICATION

Loving thanks to my family and special friends for their loyal support and encouragement, especially

Robert, Albert, and Doris

ACKNOWLEDGMENTS

Many thanks to Connie Kallback, Acquisitions Editor in Education, Prentice Hall, without whose patient guidance, practical help, and outstanding ability to track down myriad items, a difficult task would have been much more so.

Sincere appreciation for the cooperation of Jacqueline Roulette, Production Editor, Prentice Hall; and for the meticulous attention to details given by Jeanette Ninas Johnson, Editorial Director, PRI Communications, Inc.; and to all behind-the-scenes workers on this project.

Deep acknowledgement of the professional opinions and suggestions given by Diane Larson and Connie Fernández.

Finally, a heartfelt thank-you to my son, Robert, whose unstinted help eased my path; and to José González-Roig for his diligent proofreading.

ABOUT THE AUTHOR

Josephine Carreño has taught Spanish for twenty-two years on the high school and college levels: Holy Cross High School, Bayside N.Y.; Queens College, Flushing, N.Y.; and Queensborough Community College, Bayside, N.Y., where she taught until the 1994 spring semester, retiring to devote her time to writing. She has coauthored and published two books: *Spanish for Hospital Personnel* and *Spanish: Practical Communication for Health Professionals*

Her teaching experience also encompasses seminars, adult education programs, language labs, special instruction to hospital personnel and business groups, and private teaching.

She has an M.A. in Spanish from Queens College, and completed all course requirements for a Ph.D. in Spanish at New York University.

ABOUT THIS RESOURCE

This resource has been prepared to assist you, the Spanish teacher—in upper primary grades, high school, beginning college, and adult education—to help build students' comprehension and conversational skills in practical, everyday situations. The aim is to make the learning process of a foreign language pertinent, alive, and stimulating; to give a sense of accomplishment; and to encourage continued effort in expanding knowledge of the contemporary Spanish-speaking world and its culture.

You can shape the lessons to your individual teaching style and to the needs of students in particular classes. To this end, the activities are labeled "A" for beginning students or those who haven't had much experience with Spanish and "B" for more advanced students. These are loosely categorized. Since student levels differ in each class, a puzzle or activity labeled "A" may be more appropriate for a "B" level student, and vice versa. You, of course, will make the decision as to what to assign to whom.

The book contains seventeen sections, beginning with cultural information on a few Spanish-speaking countries in Section One to encourage students to expand their knowledge in this area through reading and travel.

Section Two, on cognates—words that are similar or identical in spelling and meaning in both languages—provides a giant, easy step toward the acquisition of an extensive vocabulary. Look for cognates to enhance comprehension. ¡OJO! Students should be well drilled in the differences in pronunciation and syllable-stress of Spanish-English cognates. In Spanish the vowel sounds are:

> **a (ah) e (eh) i (ēe) o (aw) u (ōo)**
> **Spanish: fatal (fah-<u>tahl</u>)**
> **English: fatal (<u>fay</u>-tŭl)**

The single sound of the Spanish vowel differs from the dipthongal sound of the English vowel.

Although, by and large, Spanish and English sentence structure runs along the same lines, some students are not well grounded in English grammar. Section Three, Parts of Speech, may help you in bolstering students' weak areas; we know how important it is to be grammatically well-versed in one's own language to make the study of a foreign language much easier.

Section Four, a short section on nouns, is included because of the importance of learning the gender of nouns since all modifiers must agree both in number and gender. Some students have a little difficulty with this concept since it does not exist in English.

Synonyms and antonyms, Section Five, will give students some fun in translating these pairs which, coincidentally, are excellent vocabulary builders.

Prefixes and suffixes in Section Six provide practice in deciphering the meaning of words that may be incomprehensible at first glance.

Section Seven on pitfalls (*trampas*) will be helpful to students in avoiding malapropisms. It focuses on expressions that have a certain meaning that is not a word-for-word translation. For example, the idiom "echar de menos"—to miss someone or something—literally translated is "to fling of less." The section also cites some commonly made errors, which may be avoided when explained:

Prefiero el libro rojo.   I prefer the red book.

Él prefiere el blanco.   He prefers the white one.

NOT "el blanco uno"

Additional practice in translation can be found in Section Eight, Proverbs (*Refranes*), beginning with an explanation of proverbs or common sayings. It includes a teacher page of proverbs that can be dictated in either English or Spanish for students to translate.

Each of the subsequent sections, 9 through 17, is based on a particular element of everyday life: food, home and family, travel, automobiles, dining in a restaurant, shopping, visiting the dentist and the doctor, with the final section focusing on sports.

Each section is enlivened with word games, puzzles, translations, and extensive vocabulary for each subject. You may want to give an assignment to two or more students to prepare a conversation on a given topic to present in class. Everyone can then participate by commenting, agreeing, disagreeing, or even ad-libbing a personal experience. This exercise can spark a lively give-and-take.

The dialogues throughout are aimed at developing conversational skills. To make them come alive, you can assign memorization of the dialogues and have students act them out in class.

¡QUÉ SE DIVIERTAN! Have fun!

Josephine Carreño

CONTENTS

ABOUT THIS RESOURCE   v

SECTION 1: LANGUAGE AND GEOGRAPHIC CHARACTERISTICS

1-1   **Why Spanish?**   3

1-2   **¿Dónde se habla español? (Background)**   4

1-3   **Differences Between Castilian and New World Spanish (Background)**   5

1-4   **Spanish-Speaking Countries**   6

1-5   **Rivers and Cities of Spain (A)**   12

1-6   **Países de habla española (A)**   13

1-7   **Find the Errors (A)**   14

1-8   **Eight Straight; One Scrambled (A)**   16

1-9   **Spanish-Speaking Countries and Their Capitals (A)**   17

1-10   **All Beginning with "al . . ." (A)**   19

SECTION 2: COGNADOS (COGNATES)

2-1   **Recognizing Cognates: Translate "Un horrible accidente" (B)**   23

2-2   **Cognates: Basic Accent Rules in Spanish (Background)**   24

2-3   **Translate: Cognates Ending in "-cto" (B)**   25

2-4   **"-cto" Endings (A)**   26

2-5   **Translate: "-ist" Endings (B)**   27

2-6   **"One Who": Word Puzzle (A)**   28

2-7   **Translate: From "-ty" to "-dad" (B)**   29

2-8   **Spanish Cognates for "-ity" Endings (A)**   30

2-9   **Buscapalabras: "-dad" Words (A)**   31

2-10   **"-tion" Cognates (A/B)**   32

2-11   **A Prize for the Most! "-ción" Cognates (A/B)**   33

2-12   "-ce" Endings to "-cia" (A)   34

2-13   Turn Around: Spanish to English (A)   35

2-14   Buscapalabras: Find the Mystery Word! (A/B)   36

2-15   Adjective to Adjective (A)   37

2-16   Buscapalabras: Mystery Word! (B)   38

2-17   More Cognates: English for Spanish (A)   39

2-18   Spanish for English (B)   40

2-19   Spanish "-oso/a" to English "-ous" (B)   41

2-20   "-ous" in Action (B)   42

2-21   "-in" to "-ina" or "-ino" (A)   43

2-22   Just ADD "-e" (A)   44

2-23   English "-ate" Verbs to Spanish "-ar" Verbs (A/B)   45

2-24   Figure Me Out! (B)   46

2-25   Watch Out! ¡Falsos amigos! (B)   47

2-26   Más falsos amigos (Vocabulary) (A/B)   49

SECTION 3: PARTS OF SPEECH

3-1   Parts of Speech (Background)   53

3-2   ¿Cómo se dice en español? (B)   56

3-3   Find Me! (A)   57

3-4   A Little Word BUT ¡Cuidado! (Be Careful!) (A)   59

3-5   I'll Take These (A/B Teacher Page)   60

SECTION 4: SUSTANTIVOS (NOUNS AND CARDINAL NUMBERS)

4-1   Sustantivos: Género, número, concordancia
(Background/Vocabulary)   63

4-2   Diálogo: Una familia cariñosa (B)   66

4-3   ¿Masculino o femenino? (A/B)   67

4-4   Tres cosas (A)   69

4-5   Números: Unas indicaciones más (A/B)   71

4-6   Read the Star (B)   73

Section 5: Sinónimos y Antónimos (Synonyms and Antonyms)

5-1   ¡Busque el sinónimo! (A/B)   77

5-2   Match Me with Another Adjective in English (A)   78

5-3   Describe Me (B)   79

5-4   Find My Noun Mate (A)   80

5-5   The Right Noun, Please (B)   81

5-6   Sustantivos opuestos (B)   82

5-7   Mystery Nouns (B)   83

5-8   Verb Antonyms (A)   84

5-9   Class Contest (A/B)   84

5-10   Adjective Antonyms (A)   85

5-11   Tell Me the Truth, Please (A/B Teacher Page)   86

Section 6: Prefijos y sufijos (Prefixes and Suffixes)

6-1   Prefixes (Vocabulary)   89

6-2   Complete the Words (A)   91

6-3   Look-alikes but Different (B)   92

6-4   Suffixes (Vocabulary)   93

6-5   ¡Juguemos "Olé"! (Let's Play "Olé"!) (A/B)   95

Section 7: Trampas (Pitfalls)

7-1   Pitfalls (Trampas) (Background)   99

7-2   ¿Dónde está? (A)   104

7-3   ¡Compléteme! (B)   105

7-4   Idioms (Background/Vocabulary)   106

7-5   ¿Cómo se dice? (Diálogo) (A)   108

SECTION 8: REFRANES (PROVERBS)

8-1   Refranes (Background) (A/B)   111

8-2   Proverbs   112

8-3   Refranes de sabiduría (A)   113

8-4   ¡Busque usted mi otra parte! (B)   114

8-5   Sabiduría en inglés y en español (Teacher's Page)   115

8-5   Sabiduriá en inglés y en español (B)   116

SECTION 9: ALIMENTOS (FOOD)

9-1   Amor y calorías (Diálogo)   119

9-2   "Cierto" es más fácil que "Falso" (B)   120

9-3   Diálogo: El hambre es la mejor salsa (A)   121

9-4   ¡Sea honesto/a! (A)   122

9-5   Es verdad (B)   123

9-6   Consejo (B)   124

9-7   Out of One, Many (B)   125

9-8   Se me hace la boca agua (My Mouth Waters) (Vocabulary)   126

9-9   Look, Ma, All Vegetables! (A/B)   127

9-10   Frutas (Vocabulary)   128

9-11   Colores (A)   129

9-12   Find the Meat and Poultry (A)   130

9-13   Shell Me (A)   131

9-14   Other Foods (Vocabulary)   132

9-15   Ahora, le toca a usted (A)   134

9-16   ¿Lo sabe usted? (B)   135

9-17   Más alimentos (A)   136

9-18   La paella valenciana—¡rica! (A)   137

9-19 ¡Ponga la mesa para el desayuno! (A)   138

9-20 ¡Arrégleme! (B)   139

9-21 ¿Perder, ganar o mantener? (B)   141

9-22 A algunos les gusta nadar (A)   142

9-23 No pertenece (A)   143

9-24 ¡Fiesta! (B)   144

9-25 ¿Qué se compra? (A)   146

9-26 ¿Qué vas a preparar? (B)   147

SECTION 10: HOGAR Y FAMILIA (HOME AND FAMILY)

10-1 Conozca usted a la familia hispana (Vocabulario, nota cultural y traduccíon)   151

10-2 ¿Quién es? (A)   153

10-3 Una merienda campestre (Diálogo y vocabulario)   154

10-4 La familia González (B)   156

10-5 Ir de camping (B)   157

10-6 ¡Olé! (A/B)   158

10-7 ¿Para qué sirve? (B)   159

10-8 Más utensilios (A/B)   160

10-9 Cuartos, muebles y componentes de una casa (B)   161

10-10 Díme . . . (A)   162

10-11 Los quehaceres domésticos (con cierto o falso) (A)   163

10-12 ¿Dónde está mi lugar? (B)   165

10-13 ¡Búsqueme! (B)   166

10-14 School and Study (Vocabulary)   167

10-15 Traduzca: El primer día del semestre (B)   168

10-16 School and Study (A/B)   169

10-17 Rompecabezas: Palabras escolásticas (B)   170

Section 11: Viajar (Travel)

11-1   ¡Buen viaje! (Background)   173

11-2   Vocabulario turístico (A)   174

11-3   Un viaje de novios (B)   175

11-4   Stopping Places in Spanish-Speaking Countries (A)   177

11-5   Diálogo: En el hotel (B)   178

11-6   Crucigrama (A)   179

11-7   Quisiera ir . . . (B)   180

Section 12: Autómoviles (Automobiles)

12-1   Alquilar un auto (A)   183

12-2   Partes del auto (B)   184

12-3   Good-Driving Rules (B)   185

12-4   Herramientas útiles (A)   186

12-5   ¿Qué pasa con mi coche? (Conversación) (A/B)   187

12-6   Señales de carreteras (A/B)   188

Section 13: Comemos en un restaurante (Dining in a Restaurant)

13-1   Food Notes (Background)   191

13-2   Un menú del restaurante "Buen Provecho" (A)   192

13-3   Diálogo: ¡No lo podemos creer! (B)   193

13-4   La palabra apropiada (A)   195

13-5   Trabalenguas (A/B)   196

Section 14: Ir de compras (Shopping in a Department Store)

14-1   Diálogo: Se equivocó (B)   199

14-2   Las tiendas (The Stores)   201

14-3 Más prendas de vestir (More Articles of Clothing) (A/B)   202

14-4 Mystery Word(s) (A/B)   203

Section 15: Consultar al dentista (Consulting a Dentist)

15-1 Diálogo: Tengo dolor de muela (B)   207

15-2 ¡Compléteme! (A)   208

15-3 ¿Qué le pasa? (B)   209

15-4 See Who Rates the Highest (B)   210

Section 16: Consultar al médico (Consulting a Doctor)

16-1 Parts of the Body (A/B)   213

16-2 Point . . . (A/B)   214

16-3 Diálogo: Pequeñas amígdalas, grandes problemas (B)   215

16-4 ¡Búsqueme y tradúzcame! (B)   216

16-5 Enfermedades (B)   217

16-6 ¡Compléteme! (B)   218

16-7 Diálogo: ¿TV o no TV?—es la pregunta (A/B)   219

16-8 Ouch! (A)   220

Section 17: Deportes (Sports)

17-1 Deportes (Sports) (A/B)   223

17-2 Identifique usted el deporte (Identify the Sport) (A)   226

17-3 ¡Búsqueme—en español! (A)   227

17-4 ¡Juguemos! (Let's Play!) (B)   228

17-5 Deportes (B)   229

ANSWER KEY   231

Section 1

LANGUAGE
AND
GEOGRAPHIC CHARACTERISTICS

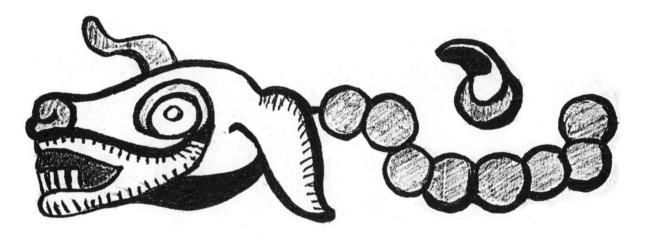

WHY

Spanish culture is part of the American heritage. The Spanish king and queen—Ferdinand and Isabel—made it possible for Columbus to discover this continent where

Professional opportunities abound if you have a knowledge of Spanish: in the United Nations organization, the Peace Corps, foreign service. It is a plus for pilots and other airline personnel. Translators in many fields are much in demand. You are an

Ambassador of good will when you travel to Spanish-speaking countries because it is in the

National interest if you can communicate in the language of the host country. This promotes better

International understanding. In addition, the

Skills you develop in mastering Spanish will help you to learn any other foreign language you may wish to study. The Spanish language can provide pleasure at

Home also. Because of the many Spanish-speaking people in the United States there are a number of entertaining and educational Spanish programs on television.

?

1-2 ¿DÓNDE SE HABLA ESPAÑOL?
(Background)

More than three hundred million people worldwide speak Spanish. In addition to Spain and its overseas provinces, the Spanish-speaking locations are:

Argentina	El Salvador	Panama
Bolivia	Dominican Republic	Paraguay
Chile		
Colombia	Guatemala	Peru
Costa Rica	Honduras	Puerto Rico
Cuba	Mexico	Uruguay
Ecuador	Nicaragua	Venezuela

Spanish is also spoken in the Philippines, in certain areas of North Africa, in the southwestern United States, and in other concentrated areas in the United States such as New York City and Miami, Florida.

4

1-3 DIFFERENCES BETWEEN CASTILIAN AND NEW WORLD SPANISH (Background)

In the New World, the Spanish language adopted many words from the regional Indian dialects, some of which remained in the area of origin; others spread throughout Latin America, and some even found their way to the mother country, Spain: examples—chocolate, huracán (hurricane), maíz (corn), tomate (tomato), and others. The Spanish language is not completely uniform. According to linguists, uniformity does not exist in any language.

However, there are basic grammatical rules that apply to both Castilian and Latin American Spanish. By and large, both have the same pronunciation, with one noticeable exception. In Castilian the sound of the "z" and that of the "c" before "i" and "e" are given the sound of "th" instead of the Latin American "s."

You will notice minor differences in accent, idioms, and vocabulary among Spanish-speaking countries. For example, in Puerto Rico the final "s" in a syllable is aspirated so that "español" is pronounced "ehpañol." The Cubans and Santo Domingans have a tendency of eliding the "d" between vowels so that "cansado" would emerge as "cansao." (Strangely enough, in some parts of Spain this irregularity is also practiced.) Also the sounds of the "r" and the "l" are frequently interchanged. Some Argentinians have their own particular way of pronouncing the "ll" and the "y" as "zh." "Yo me llamo Guillermo" would sound like "Zho me zhamo Guizhermo." Isn't variety the spice of life, though?

Some regionalisms are not accepted by Spanish dictionaries; nevertheless, they are in use. Familiarity with a few of these differences will widen one's Spanish comprehension level.

ENGLISH	CUBAN	PUERTO RICAN	MEXICAN
hole	hueco	roto	agujero
ring	anillo	sortija	anillo
truck	camión	troc	camión
tray	bandeja	azafate	charola
ear of corn	mazorca de maíz	mazorca de maíz	elote
sandals *	chancletas; sandalias	chancletas	huaraches
orange (fruit)	naranja	china	naranja
banana	banana	guineo	plátano
bedroom	cuarto	dormitorio	recámara
refrigerator	refrigerador	nevera	refrigerador
grocery store	bodega	colmado	tienda de comestibles
bathtub	bañadera	bañera	tina

*In Spain—alpargatas.

© 1996 by the Center for Applied Research in Education

1-4 SPANISH-SPEAKING COUNTRIES

SPAIN

Spain has seventeen autonomous regions. *

Andalucía	Extremadura
Aragón	Galicia
Asturias	Madrid
Baleares (Balearic Islands)	Murcia
Canarias (Canary Islands)	Navarra
Cantábria	País Vasco
Castilla León	La Rioja
Castilla la Mancha	Valencia
Cataluña	

IMPORTANT CITIES

Madrid (capital; central; established in 1561)

Barcelona (northeast; on the Mediterranean; principal port of Spain)

Valencia (east; Mediterranean coast; main exports are wine, oranges, and rice)

Bilbao (seaport in northern Spain, near Bay of Biscay; noted for its mining industry)

Sevilla (southwest; main city of Andalucía; a port on the Guadalquivir; site of the Alcázar)

Granada (south; last stronghold of the Moors in Spain; site of the Alhambra)

Toledo (central, on the bank of the river Tajo; home of the great artist, El Greco)

Cádiz (southwest; a port on the Atlantic Ocean)

Burgos (ancient capital of Castilla la Vieja, in northern Spain; home of the famous Gothic cathedral of the same name, where lies the tomb of the national hero of Spain, El Cid Campeador)

Santiago de Compostela (northwest, pilgrimage center—the tomb of the patron saint of Spain, the apostle Saint James)

Salamanca (west; site of the oldest university in Europe, built in the thirteenth century)

Córdoba (south, on the banks of the Guadalquivir)

* According to the latest known changes.

1-4 SPANISH-SPEAKING COUNTRIES *(continued)*

MOUNTAINS

Los Pirineos (north, frontier between Spain and France)

Los Cantábricos (north)

La Sierra de Gredos (center)

La Sierra de Guadarrama (center)

La Sierra Morena (south)

La Sierra Nevada (south)

El Cerro de Mulhacén (south; highest peak in Spain)

MAIN RIVERS

El Tajo (to the west; crosses Portugal; longest river in Spain)

El Duero (to the west; crosses Portugal)

El Guadiana (to the west; crosses Portugal)

El Ebro (to the north)

El Guadalquivir (to the south; the most navigable river in Spain)

LANGUAGES

Español, also called *castellano*. Derived from the Latin language of the Romans who occupied the Iberian Peninsula from 206 B.C. to 409 A.D. There is a good deal of Spanish in the English spoken in the United States. From the old Spanish territories which today form the states of California, New Mexico, Arizona, Nevada, Utah, and Texas, we have absorbed many Spanish words: adobe, alameda, alfalfa, alpaca, banana, barbecue (barbacoa), bonanza, burro, canoe (canoa), cargo, corral, chinchilla, chocolate, coyote, fiesta, hacienda, mosquito, parasol, plaza, rodeo, sierra, siesta, tobacco (tabaco), hammock (hamaca).

Gallego, a dialect spoken in Galicia; resembles Portuguese (a Romance language spoken in Portugal and Brazil). The Gallegos are descendents of the Celtic race.

Catalán, spoken in Cataluña. It resembles Provençal, a vernacular spoken in the southern part of France. Catalán is considered a Romance language that goes back to medieval times.

Vascuence, language of the Basques of *las Provincias Vascongadas*. Basque is a very ancient tongue which goes back very far, but is of unknown origin.

NOTE: Castilian (Spanish) is also spoken in all of the above areas.

OVERSEAS PROVINCES

Las islas Baleares (in the Mediterranean)

Las islas Canarias (in the Atlantic)

Various provinces in Northwest Africa

1-4 SPANISH-SPEAKING COUNTRIES (*continued*)

SOUTH AMERICA

South America has nine Spanish-speaking republics and one Portuguese-speaking (Brazil).

REPUBLIC	CAPITAL
Argentina	Buenos Aires
Bolivia (rich in minerals; tin is its most important product.)	La Paz
(Brazil)	(Brasilia)
Chile	Santiago
Colombia (the only country in South America which has ports in two oceans—the Caribbean and the Pacific)	Bogotá
Ecuador (The equator crosses it; hence its name. The equator is an imaginary line which divides the world into two hemispheres—north and south.)	Quito
Peru (Silver and copper are its two most important minerals.)	Lima
Paraguay	Asunción
Uruguay (smallest republic in South America)	Montevideo
Venezuela	Caracas

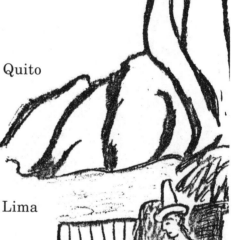

MOUNTAINS

Los Andes

MAIN RIVERS

El Amazonas (Amazon, mainly in Brazil, carries more water than any river in the world.)

El Orinoco (in Venezuela)

El Río de la Plata (in Argentina)

El Río Magdalena (in Colombia)

1-4 SPANISH-SPEAKING COUNTRIES (continued)

CENTRAL AMERICA

Central America has six republics.

REPUBLIC	CAPITAL
Costa Rica	San José
Guatemala	Guatemala City
Honduras	Tegucigalpa
Panama (a link between North and South America. In 1914 the United States completed construction of the Panama canal).*	Panama City
Nicaragua	Managua
El Salvador	San Salvador

MEXICO

In 1846 a frontier dispute started a two-year war between Mexico and the United States, as a result of which Mexico lost almost one-half of her territory, i.e., what is now California, Arizona, Nevada, Utah, New Mexico, Texas, and part of Colorado (see Note on following page).

In 1521 Hernán Cortés conquered Mexico after attacking Tenochitlán (now Mexico City), destroying it almost completely. He took as prisoner Cuauhtémoc, the last Aztec emperor.

CAPITAL

Distrito Federal (Mexico City)

OCEANS

Pacific Ocean (west coast)

Gulf of Mexico (east coast)

MOUNTAINS

Sierra Madre Occidental (to the west)

Sierra Madre Oriental (to the east)

VOLCANOES

Popocatépetl (south central)

Iztaccíhuatl (west central)

*The Panama Canal extends southeast from the Atlantic to the Pacific Ocean across the Isthmus of Panama; it is forty miles long.

Paricutín (west central)

Pico de Orizaba (northeast, the highest peak in
Mexico; more than 18,000 feet high; also
called Citlaltépetl)

*Note: Cities in the U.S., with Spanish names: El Paso, Pueblo,
San Diego, San Francisco, Santa Fe, Las Cruces, Las Vegas, San
Antonio, Sacramento, Santa Cruz, Los Angeles, and others.*

PUERTO RICO

An island commonwealth in the West Indies, Puerto Rico is called
"Borinquen" by its natives. It was discovered by Christopher Columbus in
1493 on his second voyage to the New World and remained under Spanish
rule until the end of the 19th century. Ponce de León was its first governor.
As a result of the War of 1898 between Spain and the United States, Spain
ceded the island to the United States, together with the Philippine Islands.
Until 1948 the governors of Puerto Rico were chosen by the President of the
United States. In 1948 Luis Muñoz Marín was elected governor by the Puerto
Ricans. In 1952 it was established as a free Commonwealth. Its capital is San
Juan.

CUBA

Cuba was discovered by Christopher Columbus in 1492; it lies at the entrance
to the Gulf of Mexico, and is the largest island in the West Indies. In 1899 it
was established as an independent republic. Its capital is Havana.

MOUNTAINS

Sierra Maestra

Sierra de los Órganos

Sierra de Trinidad

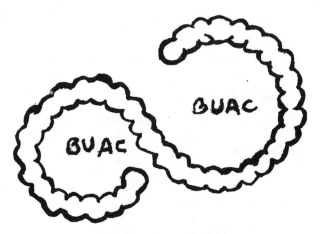

¿Cuál país es éste?

1-4 SPANISH-SPEAKING COUNTRIES *(continued)*

DOMINICAN REPUBLIC

Located in the West Indies, the Dominican Republic occupies the eastern part of the island of Hispaniola. Its capital is Santo Domingo. Historically it has withstood major conflicts. Its main export is sugar.

1-5 RIVERS AND CITIES OF SPAIN

According to the length of each line (compared with the length of the printed name) write the names of the five main rivers of Spain.

1. _____

2. _____

3. _____

4. _____

5. _____

Write the names of 12 important cities in Spain, in alphabetical order.

6. _____

7. _____

8. _____

9. _____

10. _____

11. _____

12. _____

13. _____

14. _____

15. _____

16. _____

17. _____

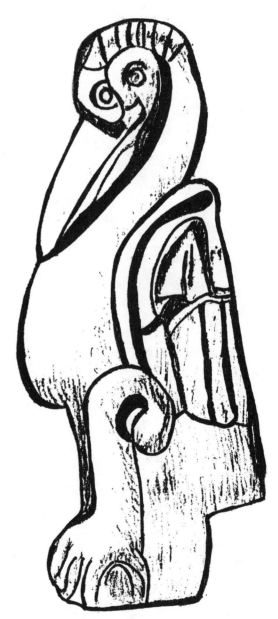

1-6 Países de habla española
(Spanish-speaking Countries)

From the underlined set of words see how many four-letter words you can extract. We lined up 65. Please follow these rules:

1. No proper names

2. No "n" for the "ñ" in the title

3. No "ll" for the two "l's" in the title

4. No duplicate letters unless there are two or more in the title

5. With each word give its part of speech, i.e., n., adj., v., etc. If it is a verb form, give the infinitive from which it derives.

6. Give the meaning of the word.

Examples: alas (n., wings)
debo (v., I should, "deber")
leal   (adj., loyal)

GO TO IT ! ! !

1-7 FIND THE ERRORS

Some of the following sentences have a mistake in the "fact" underlined. If the statement is correct, mark it "Sí." If it is incorrect, mark it "No" and rewrite the sentence with the correction.

Example:

1. **El río <u>más caudaloso</u>* del mundo es <u>el Río de la Plata</u>.**   **<u>No</u>**

   <u>El río más caudaloso del mundo es el Amazonas.</u>

2. <u>El Uruguay</u> es un país en <u>la América Central.</u>   ___

   _____

3. El catalán se habla en las <u>Provincias Vascongadas.</u>   ___

   _____

4. La capital de Colombia es <u>Bogotá.</u>   ___

   _____

5. Valencia es un puerto en <u>el Océano Pacífico.</u>   ___

   _____

6. El primer encuentro entre Cristóbal Colón y el Nuevo Mundo
   ocurrió en el <u>siglo catorce.</u>   ___

   _____

7. Cuba está en el <u>Océano Pacífico.</u>   ___

   _____

8. España tiene <u>tres</u> regiones.   ___

   _____

9. Los Andes están en <u>Sudamérica.</u>   ___

   _____

10. <u>El Distrito Federal</u> es la capital de México.   ___

    _____

* Carrying most water.

11. Puerto Rico es un <u>estado libre asociado.</u>   —

_____

12. El volcán Popocatépetl está en <u>Sudamérica.</u>   —

_____

13. <u>El Duero</u> es el río más largo de España.   —

_____

14. <u>El Paraguay</u> es la república más pequeña de Sudamérica.   —

_____

15. <u>Ponce de León</u> fue el primer gobernador de Puerto Rico.   —

_____

1-8 EIGHT SRAIGHT; ONE SCRAMBLED

In the "buscapalabras" find the names of 9 regions of Spain. Three names have 6 letters each; 5 names have 8 letters each; one name has 11 letters but they are scrambled. What is it? The names can run vertically, horizontally, backward, or forward. Circle them and write them on the lines provided under the word square.

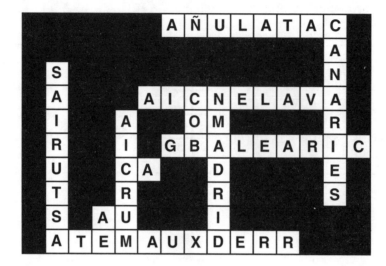

_____   _____

_____   _____

_____   _____

_____   _____

Scrambled name: _____

1-9 SPANISH-SPEAKING COUNTRIES AND THEIR CAPITALS

The word square (buscapalabras) contains 20 Spanish-speaking countries and their capitals. Their letters run vertically, horizontally (backward or forward), or diagonally (also backward or forward).

¡BÚSQUELOS! (Find them!) Circle each name in the word square; then list each country with its capital on the lines provided.

© 1996 by the Center for Applied Research in Education

	S	T	E	G	U	C	I	G	A	L	P	A	P	M	A	N	A	G	U	A	R	S	O	
C		A	T	O	G	O	B	W	V	U	A	N	O	I	C	N	U	S	A	E	L	A		R
O	N		O	P	Q	R	T	U	E	M	N	R	O	D	A	U	C	E	P	C	A		S	L
L	O	M	N	S	A	C	A	R	A	C	A	Y	P	E	R	U	R	U	S	I	R	S	M	I
O	L	A	L	A	M	E	T	A	U	G	M	E	L	B	C	D	B	R	A	S	E	A	O	M
M	E	X	I	C	O	O	N	U	X	Y	A	Z	T	C	F	L	G	H	N	A	D	N	N	A
B	D	G	D	I	R	D	A	M	H	I	J	L	N	K	I	P	O	A	T	N	E	J	T	O
I	L	S	L	I	M	A	T	W	V	X		O		C	U	N	Y	V	I	T	F	O	E	R
A	I	K	C	Q	U	W	S	A	N	M	O		A	N	D	B	T	A	A	O	O	S	V	O
A	D	O	E	L	A	P	A	Z	J	L		D		U	A	M	I	N	G	D	T	E	I	D
N	Q	U	C	R	U	T	Q	U	I	T	O	I	R	S	L	T	C	A	O	O	I	Q	D	A
I	S	C	O	A	U	N	V	O	W	M	L	A	M	A	E	L	A	N	K	M	R	C	E	V
T	U	M	S	M	R	S	E	R	I	A	S	O	N	E	U	B	M	A	S	I	T	H	O	L
N	T	X	T	A	U	W	V	N	B	D	F	H	I	J	Z	K	A	U	M	N	S	I	N	A
E	J	X	A	N	G	O	I	B	O	L	I	V	I	A	E	G	N	J	H	G	I	L	J	S
G	W	N	R	A	U	C	A	U	G	A	R	A	C	I	N	M	A	N	L	O	D	E	K	N
R	X		I	P	A	R	A	G	U	A	Y	J	L	K	E	S	P	A	Ñ	A	L		M	A
A		N	C	N	Y	O	P	R	S	T	R	O	D	A	V	L	A	S	L	E	W	O		S
	D	E	A	B	U	C	K	U	G	U	A	T	E	M	A	L	A	C	I	T	Y	E	R	

SPANISH-SPEAKING COUNTRIES AND THEIR CAPITALS

1. _____

2. _____

3. _____

4. _____

5. _____

6. _____

7. _____

8. _____

9. _____

10. _____

11. _____

12. _____

13. _____

14. _____

15. _____

16. _____

17. _____

18. _____

19. _____

20. _____

1-10 ALL BEGINNING WITH "AL..."

The word square contains 20 words—all nouns and all beginning with "al-." They are positioned either horizontally or vertically. Circle them on the word square; then write them on the lines provided. Give the gender of each noun—m. or f.—and give the meaning. Look for those friendly cognates (words that are similar, or almost similar, to English in spelling and similar in meaning).

```
        C A L                        A L C A Z A R T J
        O L E                        L A M L O L Q R V
        J U C A                      B E F H G I K M N
        A C O L                      U X U A M V N P C
      S L T H U L                    M E X J C I O A L
      B D X O M T                    H I K A L O M O P
      X E U L N V I                  A L P A R G A T A
      M O A Z E A F J                L A M E N T O S O
        A                           U R A Z T A R E L
      A L I M E N T O S              M A L I E N T O I
      J T F O S V W X M T            I L P T W U X P B
      M C A L C A L D E R            N E X E Z X V O L
      C U B A L V E Z P T            I R E A L P A C A
  A B D E M P N A L T A R            O G A N O D E L O
  Z A L T I T U D E N S E            M I G R A N O E A
  A L M O H A D A A L M A            L A M E N T A B L
                                     B A L F O M B R A
```

1. _____   11. _____

2. _____   12. _____

3. _____   13. _____

4. _____   14. _____

5. _____   15. _____

6. _____   16. _____

7. _____   17. _____

8. _____   18. _____

9. _____   19. _____

10. _____   20. _____

COGNADOS (COGNATES)

**C
O
G
N
A
D
O
S**

2-1 RECOGNIZING COGNATES

A cognate is a word that is spelled the same—or almost the same—and has the same meaning in both English and the language you are studying; in this case, Spanish. There are hundreds of cognates in Spanish, which means that your comprehension will prove to be more extensive than you think. Consider cognates as twins of similar origin. Some are identical and some are fraternal, i.e., similar but with a slight difference.

See for yourself. Read the following incident; underline all the cognates you recognize; then write a <u>translation</u> of the occurrence on another sheet.

UN HORRIBLE ACCIDENTE

Ayer ocurrió un <u>horrible accidente</u>. Mi hermano estaba conduciendo su auto en la ciudad. Él es un chófer muy competente y muy cuidadoso. De repente (suddenly) otro automóvil pasó la luz roja y chocó (collided) con el vehículo de mi hermano. Vino el policía; pidió (asked for) la documentación de los dos conductores. El imprudente no tenía ni póliza de seguros ni otros documentos necesarios. Resultó que su auto era robado (stolen). Así, el perpetrador fue llevado a la prisión y mi hermano fue llevado al hospital porque sufrió una postración nerviosa.

2-2 COGNATES: BASIC ACCENT RULES IN SPANISH
(Background)

¡O J O!

NOTE: Since many cognates are spelled the same in both English and Spanish, it is important to give the Spanish cognate the <u>Spanish</u> pronunciation and not the English.

Example: natural—<u>năch</u>-ĕr-ŭl (English)
natural—nah-tōō-<u>rahl</u> (Spanish)

The vowels in Spanish have a pure, one-letter sound and not the diphthongal (two-letter) English pronunciation. In Spanish the vowels are pronounced:

a (ah)

e (ĕh)

i (ēē)

o (like the first part of *oh*)

u (ōō)

Also, remember these basic syllable-stress (accent) rules:

- A word ending in a consonant, EXCEPT "n" or "s," accents the last syllable: espa<u>ñol</u>.

- A word ending in a vowel or the consonants "n" or "s" accents the next-to-the-last syllable: espa<u>ño</u>la, espa<u>ño</u>las, tra<u>ba</u>jan.

- A word that does not fit in either of these two categories carries its own WRITTEN accent: diálogo, automóvil, simpática.

© 1996 by the Center for Applied Research in Education

2-3 TRANSLATE: COGNATES ENDING IN "-CTO"

There are many easy ways to pair English-Spanish cognates. For example, words that end in "-ct" can be translated into Spanish by simply adding "-o" to the "-ct" ending.

Try this approach by translating the following sentences into Spanish. Underline the words that exemplify this transition. Be aware that there are other types of cognates that will aid you in the translation.

1. The first act of the drama had one defect.

   _____

2. Albert Einstein had a great intellect.

   _____

3. The novel *Don Quijote de la Mancha* is the product of a master of satire, Miguel de Cervantes.

   _____

4. The actor had a fierce aspect. The effect on his victim was frightening (espantoso).

   _____

   _____

5. The pilot lost all contact with the airfield (campo de aviación).

   _____

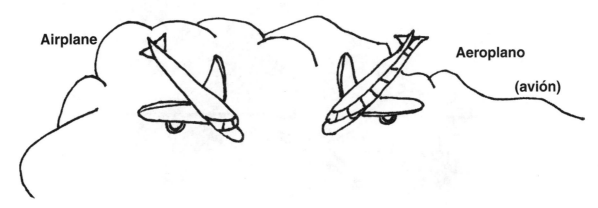

Airplane

Aeroplano

(avión)

2-4 "-CTO" ENDINGS

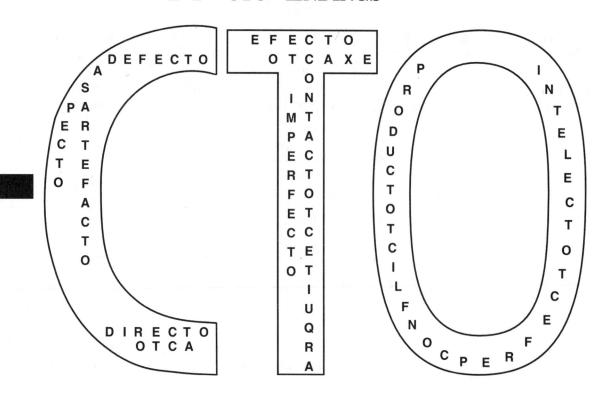

Find all the words ending in "-cto" and circle them; list them with their English cognates.

1. _____   8. _____

2. _____   9. _____

3. _____   10. _____

4. _____   11. _____

5. _____   12. _____

6. _____   13. _____

7. _____   14. _____

2-5 TRANSLATE: "-IST" ENDINGS

For nouns that end in "-ist" add an "-a" to the English "-ist" ending to form its Spanish cognate.

Note: Although these words end in "a" they can be either masculine or feminine.

Translate the following sentences into Spanish.

1. The capitalist is a person who has much money.

   _____

2. A tourist generally travels throughout the world.

   _____

3. An optimist says that the glass is half-full.

   _____

4. A pessimist says that it is half-empty.

   _____

5. Alicia De Larrocha is a great pianist.

   _____

6. Anton Rubinstein was a great pianist and composer.

   _____

7. An idealist sees everything through rose-colored glasses.

   _____

8. Diego Velásquez is an outstanding (sobresaliente) Spanish artist.

   _____

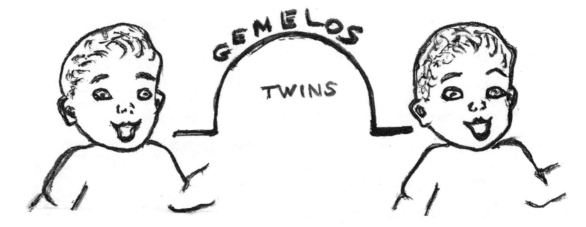

2-6 "One Who": Word Puzzle

```
I N D I V I D U A L I S T A
N   E   C O M U N I S T A T
D   N A A     A N A E T S
U A T T T     A T G T C S I
S T I S S     T U U S O I T
T S S I I     S R I I N N R
R I T T L     I A S F O I E
I S A R U     L L T I M L C
A E L A C     A I A C I O N
L R E F O R M I S T A S I O
  I G         C T   P T V C
  S N         O A     A
  T O R G A N I S T A
A C T I V I S T A T S I E D
```

In the word square, circle words that mean "one who...." Write them next to their proper definition.

1. One who takes care of your teeth _____

2. One who takes care of your eyes _____

3. One who specializes in money matters _____

4. One who advocates communism _____

5. One who advocates socialism _____

6. One who plays the organ _____

7. One who believes in peace _____

8. One who plays the violin _____

9. One who believes in a God who created the world _____

10. One who performs a musical solo _____

11. One who is a member of Congress _____

12. One who works for reforms _____

13. One who specializes in languages _____

14. One who manages an industrial enterprise _____

15. One who believes in living his own life in his own way _____

16. One who, through action, hopes to fulfill a political goal _____

17. One who studies nature _____

18. One who devotes his life to art _____

© 1996 by the Center for Applied Research in Education

2-7 TRANSLATE: FROM "-TY" TO "-DAD"

English words that end in "-ty" become Spanish cognates by substituting "-dad" for the "-ty" ending. These words are generally feminine.

Translate the following sentences into Spanish.

1. The reality of the crime was horrible.

   _____

2. Cats have a lot of curiosity.

   _____

3. Benjamin Franklin used a kite (cometa, literally, "comet") to prove that there was electricity in lightning (relámpagos).

   _____

4. They say that variety is the spice (la sazón) of life.

   _____

5. The velocity of the train caused the accident.

   _____

2-8 SPANISH COGNATES FOR "-ITY" ENDINGS

Give the Spanish cognate for the following English words.

1. authority _____
2. credibility _____
3. complexity _____
4. culpability _____
5. anxiety _____
6. felicity _____
7. improbability _____
8. impartiality _____

9. insincerity _____
10. nationality _____
11. maternity _____
12. necessity _____
13. opportunity _____
14. personality _____
15. probability _____
16. stability _____

2-9 BUSCAPALABRAS: "-DAD" WORDS

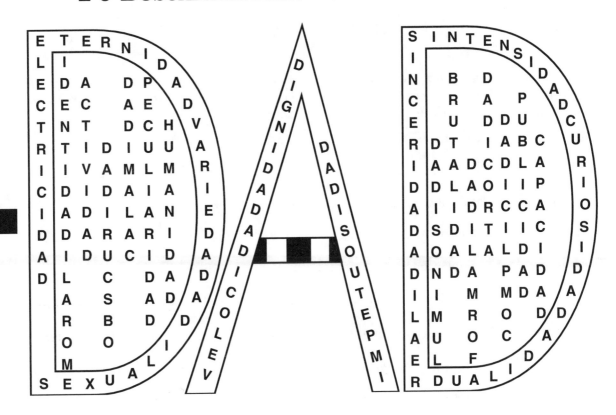

Circle all the "-dad" words you can find. List them at the bottom of the page with their English cognates. ¡Haga un buen amigo de su diccionario!

_____   _____

_____   _____

_____   _____

_____   _____

_____   _____

_____   _____

_____   _____

_____   _____

_____   _____

_____   _____

_____   _____

Nombre _____ **Fecha** _____ **(A/B)**

2-10 "-TION" COGNATES

Words that end in "-tion" in English have Spanish cognates that end in "-ción"; these are feminine in gender.

NOTE: There are no double consonants in Spanish, except "cc" (the first "c" is pronounced as "k," the second as "s") and, rarely, a double "n." The combinations "ll" (pronounced as "y") and "rr" (which has a strong trill) are considered separate letters.

Give the Spanish cognate of:

1. action _____
6. description _____

2. ambition _____
7. election _____

3. attention _____
8. emotion _____

4. celebration _____
9. intention _____

5. condition _____
10. revolution _____

Using the vocabulary listed above, <u>fill in</u> the missing words in the following sentences.

11. El alumno no prestó _____ a la maestra.

12. El 4 de julio es un día de _____ .

13. El periodista dió una _____ completa del terremoto.

14. Su _____ era fuera de la realidad.

15. La _____ humana es discutible.

16. Don Quijote era un hombre de _____ .

17. La _____ del congresista fue unánime.

18. La _____ francesa ocurrió en 1789.

19. La película nos dió una _____ de nostalgia.

20. El presidente Zedillo de México tiene la _____ de mejorar su gobierno.

2-11 A PRIZE FOR THE MOST! ("-CIÓN" COGNATES)

How many cognates can you list which end in "-tion" in English and "-ción" in Spanish?

Communication

Comunicación

2-12 "-CE" ENDINGS TO "-CIA"

Recognize easy cognates. Many words that end in "-ce" in English have Spanish cognates ending in "-cia"; these are feminine. Watch for exceptions: example—silence = silencio (masc.).

Give the Spanish cognates of the following

ENGLISH NOUNS.

1. ambulance
2. audience
3. cadence
4. competence
5. conference
6. continence
7. correspondence
8. diligence
9. distance
10. elegance
11. eminence
12. excellence
13. existence
14. independence
15. innocence
16. intelligence
17. insignificance
18. patience
19. presence
20. prudence

2-13 TURN AROUND: SPANISH TO ENGLISH

Give the English cognates of the following Spanish words.

1. continencia (moderation) _____

2. correspondencia _____

3. diferencia _____

4. elegancia _____

5. eminencia _____

6. esencia _____

7. excelencia _____

8. existencia _____

9. experiencia _____

10. insignificancia _____

11. jurisprudencia (system of laws) _____

12. magnificencia _____

13. malevolencia (malice) _____

14. paciencia _____

15. presencia _____

16. prudencia _____

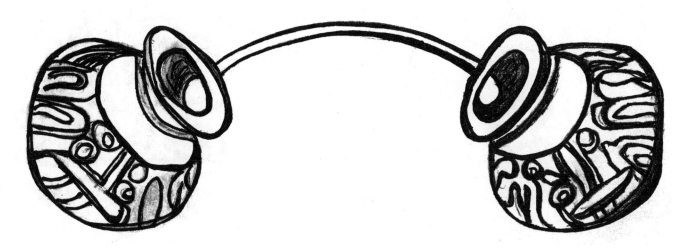

2-14 BUSCALABRAS: FIND THE MYSTERY WORD!

In the word square write the Spanish cognates for the English words listed under the square. In Spanish they all end in "-cia." The English words are given in the vertical order in which they should be placed in the square. Placed in the right boxes, the shaded area will spell a word that applies to cognates.

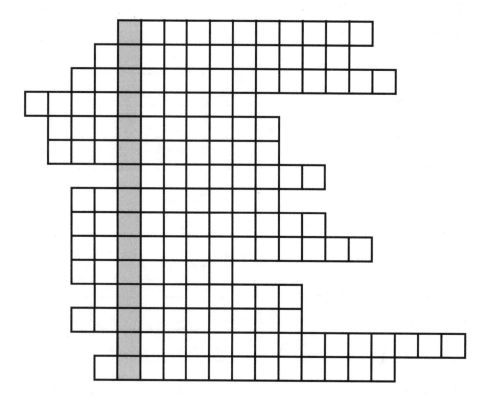

1. continence
2. competence
3. jurisprudence
4. tolerance
5. difference
6. existence
7. patience
8. violence
9. conference

10. independence
11. essence
12. innocence
13. excellence
14. insignificance
15. magnificence

Mystery word: _____

2-15 ADJECTIVE TO ADJECTIVE

Many words that end in "-ive" in English have Spanish equivalents ending in "-ivo." Since most of these words are adjectives, they have their feminine forms ending in "-iva."

Give the English cognates of the following Spanish adjectives.

1. activo (a)   _____

2. atractivo (a)   _____

3. constructivo (a)   _____

4. descriptivo (a)   _____

5. diminutivo (a)   _____

6. efectivo (a)   _____

7. exclusivo (a)   _____

8. nativo (a)   _____

9. negativo (a)   _____

10. positivo (a)   _____

11. primitivo (a)   _____

12. productivo (a)   _____

13. progresivo (a)   _____

14. superlativo (a)   _____

15. tentativo (a)   _____

2-16 BUSCALABRAS: MYSTERY WORD!

Although the "form" is feminine, the contents are masculine (taken from the list in activity 2-15). Find them, circle them, and list them at the bottom of the "-iva." One word is not given on the list. What is it?

_____   _____

_____   _____

_____   _____

_____   _____

_____   _____

_____   _____

_____   _____

_____   _____

_____   _____

_____ (Not on list)

2-17 MORE COGNATES: ENGLISH FOR SPANISH

Many words that end in "-em" or "-am" in English have their Spanish mates ending in "-ema" or "-ama."

Note: Although these words end in "-a," they are masculine.

Give the English cognate for the following Spanish words.

1. el cablegrama _____

2. el programa _____

3. el teorema (equation, formula) _____

4. el problema _____

5. el emblema _____

6. el monograma _____

7. el poema _____

8. el telegrama _____

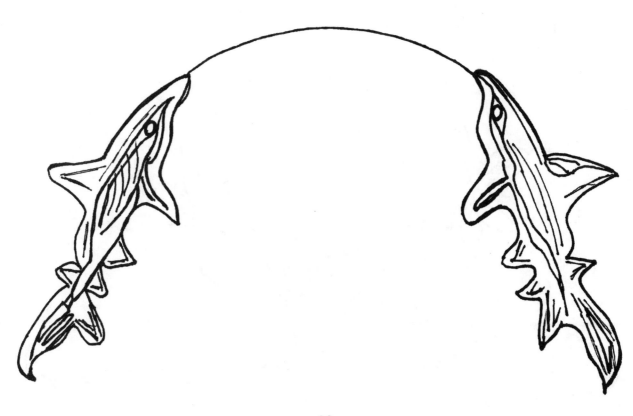

2-18 SPANISH FOR ENGLISH

Many words that end in "-ent" in English have their Spanish counterparts ending in "-ento" or "-iento."

Give the Spanish cognate for the following English words.

1. document _____

2. element _____

3. impediment _____

4. increment _____

5. ligament _____

6. movement (ie) _____

7. sacrament _____

8. sediment _____

9. sentiment (ie) _____

10. temperament _____

2-19 SPANISH "-OSO/A" TO ENGLISH "-OUS"

English words ending in "-ous" have their Spanish mates ending in "-oso" or "-osa," if it is an adjective modifying a feminine noun.

Give the Spanish equivalent of these English words.

1. ambitious _____

2. calamitous _____

3. capricious _____

4. curious _____

5. delicious _____

6. fabulous _____

7. famous _____

8. generous _____

9. impetuous _____

10. industrious _____

11. malicious _____

12. religious _____

13. victorious _____

Using the list above, complete the following Spanish cognates. The number of dashes will lead you to the right word. If there are more words than one with the same number of letters preceding the "-oso" ending, the first letter of that word is given. Give the English equivalent also.

14. __ __ __ oso (a) _____

15. __ __ __ __ __ oso (a) _____

16. g __ __ __ __ oso (a) _____

17. r __ __ __ __ __ __ oso (a) _____

18. v __ __ __ __ __ __ __ oso (a) _____

19. __ __ __ __ __ __ __ __ __ oso (a) _____

2-20 "-OUS" IN ACTION

Translate the following sentences into Spanish.

1. The victorious gladiator (gladiador) ate an abundant portion of the delicious meal prepared especially for this fabulous occasion by the king's cook (cocinero).

   _____

   _____

   _____

2. The ambitious student gets fabulous grades.

   _____

3. George Washington, the famous hero of the American Revolution, was also the first president of the United States.

   _____

   _____

   _____

4. Mother Teresa is a generous and religious person.

   _____

   _____

2-21 "-IN" TO "-INA" OR "-INO"

English words that end in "-in" or "-ine" form their Spanish cognates by replacing those endings with "-ina" or "-ino."

Write the Spanish cognates of the following words.

1. aspirin   _____

2. discipline   _____

3. gasoline   _____

4. gelatine   _____

5. medicine   _____

6. paraffin (wax) _____

7. sardine   _____

8. vitamin   _____

9. alpine   _____

10. marine   _____

11. feminine   _____

12. penguin   _____

2-22 JUST ADD "-E"

English words that end in "-ent" or "-ant" become Spanish cognates by adding "-e" to the last "-t."

Make the relationship with the following words.

1. accident _____

2. competent _____

3. constant _____

4. continent _____

5. decent _____

6. different _____ (no double "f")

7. elegant _____

8. evident _____

9. excellent _____ (no double "l")

10. important _____

11. restaurant _____

12. tolerant _____

13. vigilant _____

14. penitent _____

© 1996 by the Center for Applied Research in Education

2-23 ENGLISH "-ATE" VERBS TO SPANISH "-AR" VERBS

Here's another easy transition with many verbs that end in "-ate" in English and slide into an "-ar" ending in Spanish. Try this out with the following English verbs.

    1. alienate   _____

    2. amputate   _____

    3. appreciate   _____

    4. coagulate   _____

    5. communicate   _____ (no double "m")

    6. compensate   _____

    7. contaminate   _____

    8. debilitate   _____

    9. evaluate   _____

  10. indicate   _____

  11. implicate   _____

  12. operate   _____

  13. penetrate   _____

  14. recuperate   _____

  15. renovate   _____

  16. resuscitate   _____

2-24 FIGURE ME OUT!

Can you guess what these cognates are? The part of speech, the meaning, and the number of letters in each word are given to lead you on the right path. They are all exact cognates in English and Spanish. The first letter is also given.

1. **C** _ _ _ _ _ _ _ (noun, authority, domination) _ _ _ _ _ _ _ _

2. **O** _ _ _ _ _ _ _ _ (adj., not a copy) _ _ _ _ _ _ _ _ _

3. **G** _ _ _ _ _ _ _ (adj., common, widespread) _ _ _ _ _ _ _ _

4. **N** _ _ _ _ _ _ _ (adj., in name only) _ _ _ _ _ _ _ _

5. **A** _ _ _ _ _ (noun, heavenly being) _ _ _ _ _ _

6. **T** _ _ _ _ _ _ (noun, intense fear) _ _ _ _ _ _ _

7. **E** _ _ _ _ _ _ _ (noun, obscuring of light from a heavenly body)

   _ _ _ _ _ _ _ _

8. **S** _ _ _ _ _ _ _ _ (adj., higher in rank) _ _ _ _ _ _ _ _ _

© 1996 by the Center for Applied Research in Education

2-25 WATCH OUT! ¡FALSOS AMIGOS!

A word of caution! Some words may look like cognates, but they are not. We call them "false friends." Here are a few examples:

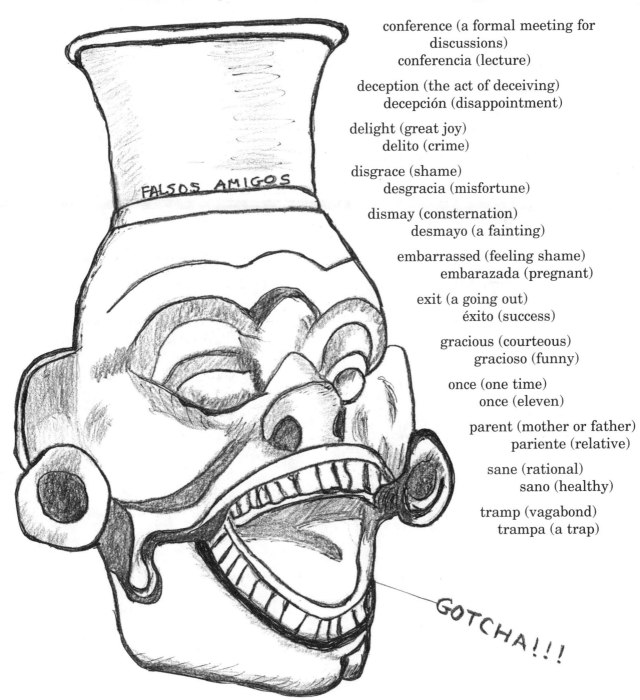

conference (a formal meeting for discussions)
conferencia (lecture)

deception (the act of deceiving)
decepción (disappointment)

delight (great joy)
delito (crime)

disgrace (shame)
desgracia (misfortune)

dismay (consternation)
desmayo (a fainting)

embarrassed (feeling shame)
embarazada (pregnant)

exit (a going out)
éxito (success)

gracious (courteous)
gracioso (funny)

once (one time)
once (eleven)

parent (mother or father)
pariente (relative)

sane (rational)
sano (healthy)

tramp (vagabond)
trampa (a trap)

Traduzca.

1. María is very embarrassed.

   _____

2. The clown's act was funny.

   _____

3. My parents are on vacation.

   _____

4. John's dog is healthy now.

   _____

5. The criminal was not sane.

   _____

6. The tramp fell into a trap.

   _____

2-26 Más falsos amigos (Vocabulary)

SPANISH	ENGLISH
actual (present-day)	actual (real)
agonía (death struggle)	agony (great mental or physical pain)
arena (sand)	arena (stadium)
asistir (to attend)	assist (to help)
atender (to attend to)	attend (to be present at)
bizarro (brave, dashing)	bizarre (strange)
campo (field)	camp (a place where temporary shelters are put up)
editor (publisher)	editor (one who arranges for publication)
emocionante (thrilling)	emotional (causing emotion)
injuria (offence)	injury (harm done)
pan (bread)	pan (cooking utensil)
recolección (compilation)	recollection (memory)
red (net)	red (color)
simpático (pleasant)	sympathetic (compassionate)

Traduzca usted las palabras entre paréntesis.

1. Hay mucha (sand _____) en la playa.

2. La película era muy (thrilling _____).

3. El profesor de español es (pleasant _____).

4. Hay una (net _____) entre los dos jugadores de tenis.

5. Se vende (bread _____) en la panadería.

6. El (field _____) de fútbol es muy grande.

PARTS OF SPEECH

The Anatomy of a Sentence: Lay down the right bricks (words) and you'll have a strong construction (sentence).

3-1 PARTS OF SPEECH (Background)

What follows is simply an outline of Spanish grammatical structure which basically goes along the same lines as in English, with some exceptions, of course. For further details and drills study your Spanish grammar textbook.

A simple sentence consist of two parts—a subject (sujeto) and a predicate (predicado)—and expresses a complete thought.

El español   **es una lengua romance.**
  (sujeto)   **(predicado)**

PARTS OF SPEECH THAT ARE USED IN A SENTENCE

A <u>noun</u> (nombre, sustantivo) can be a thing, a person, a quality. All nouns have a gender—masculine or feminine.

> **Este <u>libro</u> me pertenece. (a thing)**
> **El <u>niño</u> tiene tres años. (a person)**
> **La <u>honradez</u> es una característica deseable. (quality)**

A <u>proper noun</u> (nombre propio) can be the name of a person, an organization, a geographical area.

> **<u>Octavio Paz</u> es un famoso escritor mexicano. (a person)**
> **<u>Teléfonos de México</u> es una compañía telefónica. (an organization)**
> **Miguel de Unamuno, un gran filósofo y escritor, nació en <u>Bilbao</u>, <u>España</u>. (a geographical area)**

A <u>collective noun</u> (nombre colectivo) names a group of people or things, generally considered singular in number.

> **El <u>público</u> votó contra el candidato republicano.**

A <u>compound noun</u> (nombre compuesto) consists of two or more words.

> **El <u>abrelatas</u> (abre - latas) es un utensilio necesario en la cocina.**

A <u>pronoun</u> (pronombre) takes the place of a noun.

> **<u>Ellas</u> llegaron temprano a la fiesta.**

A <u>nominative pronoun</u> (pronombre nominativo) is the subject of a sentence or a clause.

> **<u>Nosotros</u> somos muy estudiosos. (subject of a sentence)**
>
> **Es una lástima que <u>él</u> no esté aquí. (subject of a clause)**

An <u>objective pronoun</u> (pronombre objetivo) is the object of a verb or preposition.

> **¿Los platos? <u>Los</u> puse en la mesa. (object of the verb "puse"—poner)**
> **<u>Te</u> digo la verdad. (object of the preposition "to" understood)**

3-1 PARTS OF SPEECH (Background) *(continued)*

A personal pronoun (pronombre personal) refers to a person or persons.

> **Ellos viven en Costa Rica.**

A relative pronoun (pronombre relativo) relates to a noun which precedes it in a sentence or a clause.

> **Usted es la única persona que lo sabe todo. (Refers to "persona.")**

A demonstrative pronoun (pronombre demostrativo) points to a person, place, or thing.

> **Ésa es la persona culpable. (That is the guilty person.)**
> **Éste es el lugar más deseable. (This is the most desirable place.)**
> **Ése es mi libro. (That is my book.)**

An interrogative pronoun (pronombre interrogativo) asks a question.

> **¿Quién es él? (Who is he?)**

A possessive pronoun (pronombre posesivo) indicates ownership.

> **La casa es tuya. (The house is yours.)**

An adjective (adjetivo) modifies or limits a noun.

> **El hombre alto es mi hermano. (Modifies "hombre.")**
> **Tengo diez dólares en mi bolsa. (Limits "dólares.")**

An adverb (adverbio) modifies a verb, an adjective, or another adverb.

> **El caballo corre rápidamente. (Modifies the verb "corre.")**
> **Usted es muy amable. (Modifies the adjective "amable.")**
> **El gato camina más lentamente que el perro. (Modifies the adverb "lentamente.")**

A preposition (preposición) connects a noun or pronoun to another element of a sentence: in, with, at, of, etc.

> **Madrid es la capital de España.**
> **Navarra está en la frontera con Francia.**

A conjunction (conjunción) joins words, clauses, sentences.

> **La avaricia y el egotismo son características desagradables. (Joins words.)**
> **Él contribuye dinero aunque no es miembro del club. (Joins clauses.)**
> **A él le gusta cantar y a ella le gusta bailar. (Joins sentences.)**

A verb (verbo) expresses action, state of being.

> **El río Duero atraviesa Portugal. (action)**
> **El río Tajo es el más largo de España. (state of being)**

A participle (participio) is part of a verb form. The present participle is used to form the present progressive tense, consisting of the present tense of the verb "estar" and the present participle of the main verb. With "-ar" verbs you have an "-ando" ending (caminar - caminando). With "-er" and "-ir" verbs you have an "-iendo" ending (correr - corriendo; salir - saliendo).

© 1996 by the Center for Applied Research in Education

El bebé <u>está caminando</u>. (The baby <u>is walking</u>.)
El perro <u>está corriendo</u> en la calle. (The dog <u>is running</u> in the street.)
El sol <u>está saliendo</u>. (The sun <u>is coming out</u>.)

The <u>present participle</u> is also used to form the <u>past progressive</u> tense, consisting of the imperfect tense of the verb "estar" and the present participle of the main verb.

El bebé <u>estaba caminando</u>. (The baby <u>was walking</u>.)
El perro <u>estaba corriendo</u> en la calle. (The dog <u>was running</u> in the street.)
El sol <u>estaba saliendo</u>. (The sun <u>was coming out</u>.)

The <u>past participle</u> is used to form the <u>present perfect</u> tense, consisting of the present tense of the verb "haber" and the past participle of the main verb.

Yo <u>he hablado</u>. (I <u>have spoken</u>.)
Juan <u>ha comido</u>. (John <u>has eaten</u>.)
Los precios <u>han subido</u>. (The prices <u>have gone up</u>.)

The <u>past participle</u> is also used to form the <u>pluperfect tense</u> (pluscuampersecto), consisting of the imperfect tense of the verb "haber" and the past participle of the main verb.

Yo <u>había hablado</u>. (I <u>had spoken</u>.)
Juan <u>había comido</u>. (John <u>had eaten</u>.)
Los precios <u>habían subido</u>. (The prices <u>had gone up</u>.)

3-2 ¿CÓMO SE DICE EN ESPAÑOL?

Translate the following sentences.

1. I <u>am beginning</u> to understand the problem. (pres. prog. of "empezar")

   _____

2. We <u>are learning</u> Spanish. (pres. prog. of "aprender")

   _____

3. The students <u>are writing</u> the lesson. (pres. prog. of "escribir")

   _____

4. I <u>have chatted</u> with my friends. (pres. perf. of "charlar")

   _____

5. You <u>have convinced</u> me. (pres. perf. of "convencer")

   _____

6. The workmen <u>have followed</u> the instructions. (pres. perf. of "seguir")

   _____

7. I <u>had bought</u> the book. (pluperfect of "comprar")

   _____

8. You <u>had obeyed</u> your parents. (pluperfect of "obedecer")

   _____

9. We <u>had slept</u> well. (pluperfect of "dormir")

   _____

3-3 FIND ME!

Give the part of speech of the word(s) underlined. The first sentence is done for you. Then, form a compound noun from the circled letters. Write that word on line 18.

1. **España es una nación <u>industrial</u>. (adjetivo; modifica el nombre "nación")**

2. <u>Jerez</u> y <u>Málaga</u> son ciudades célebres por sus vinos.

   _____

3. España y Portugal <u>forman</u> la Península Ibérica.

   _____

4. La ciudad <u>más</u> grande de España es Madrid.

   _____

5. <u>El Cid</u> es un héroe nacional de España.

   _____

6. Plácido Domingo <u>ha cantado</u> en muchas óperas.

   _____

7. Esta novela presenta un estudio penetrante <u>de la</u> naturaleza humana.

   _____

8. Francisco Goya fue el pintor más famoso de su <u>época</u>.

   _____

9. La música <u>que</u> acompaña al baile flamenco se produce con la guitarra.

   _____

10. La <u>gente</u> de la calle es pobre.

    _____

11. <u>Esto</u> es insoportable.

    _____

12. <u>Nosotros</u> hemos ganado el premio gordo de la lotería.

    _____

3-3 FIND ME! *(continued)*

13. Te <u>lo</u> digo yo.

_____

14. <u>Estamos pensando</u> en ti, querida mamá.

_____

15. El torero <u>y</u> el matador forman parte de la corrida.

_____

16. Los árabes <u>habían conquistado</u> a España.

_____

17. <u>Estábamos comiendo</u> cuando sonó el teléfono.

_____

18. _____

3-4 A LITTLE WORD BUT ¡CUIDADO! (BE CAREFUL!)

An article functions as an adjective.

Definite article (artículo definido)

la: **feminine, singular—la casa (the house)**
las: **feminine, plural—las casas (the houses)**
el: **masculine, singular—el libro (the book)**
los: **masculine, plural—los libros (the books)**

Indefinite article (artículo indefinido)

un: **masculine, singular—un hombre (a man)**
una: **feminine, singular—una niña**

NOTE: When the indefinite article is pluralized its meaning changes to "some" or "a few."

Manolo irá a Nueva York por <u>unos</u> días.
(Manolo will go to New York for a <u>few</u> days.)
María se quedó en Madrid por <u>unas</u> semanas.
(María stayed in Madrid for a <u>few</u> weeks.)

NON-CONFORMISTS

Some nouns do not conform to the general rule of "-o" ending for masculine, and "-a" ending for feminine. Fill in the proper definite article for the following words. If you are not sure of the gender, consult your good friend, the dictionary.

1. _____ mano   7. _____ planeta

2. _____ drama   8. _____ problema

3. _____ clima   9. _____ radio

4. _____ mapa   10. _____ idioma

5. _____ programa   11. _____ telegrama

6. _____ foto*   12. _____ moto**

*Short for "fotografía"; ** short for "motocicleta."

© 1996 by the Center for Applied Research in Education

3-5 I'll Take These (A/B Teacher Page)

Each student will:

1. Select 10 "coins."

2. Construct 10 sentences with the parts of speech indicated on that coin. Works well for homework or in-class assignment.

3. The students will correct each other's work.

As you grade the papers, you will coincidentally discover the areas that need more clarification.

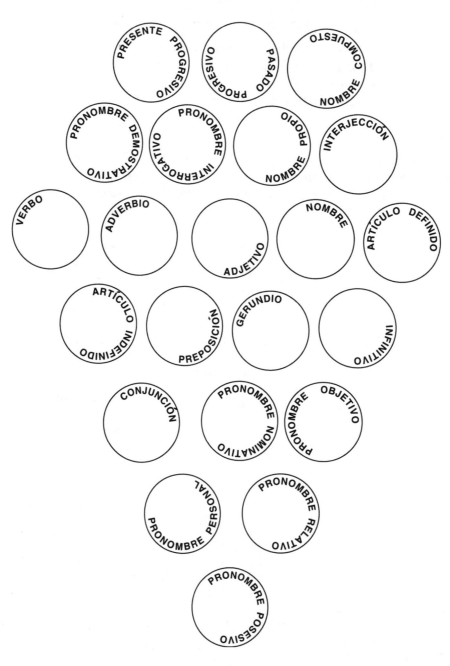

60

NOUNS AND CARDINAL NUMBERS

S
U
S
T
A
N
T
I
V
O
S

NOMBRE

GÉNERO
NÚMERO
CONCORDANCIA
(Números Cardinales)

4-1 SUSTANTIVOS: GÉNERO, NÚMERO, CONCORDANCIA (Background/Vocabulary)

All nouns in Spanish are either feminine or masculine. It is important to determine the gender and number of each noun because all its modifiers (adjectives, definite and indefinite articles) must agree in number and gender.

Generally, a noun that ends in "a" is feminine, and one that ends in "o" is masculine. Be aware that there are exceptions: la mano; el drama. Then there are nouns that end in neither "a" or "o." Learn the gender of these as you go along: el instante (the instant); la imagen (the image).

A NOUN CAN BE THE GENERAL NAME OF:

A person: el muchacho (boy); la muchacha (girl)

A place: el continente (continent); la ciudad (city)

An animal: la vaca (cow); el perro (dog)

An idea: la democracia (democracy); el socialismo (socialism)

An emotion: el amor (love); la codicia (greed)

All of the above are "common" nouns. The names of geographical places or particular people are called "proper" nouns and are always capitalized.

GUIDELINES TO HELP DETERMINE GENDER OF NOUNS THAT DO NOT END IN EITHER "A" OR "O"

Generally feminine are nouns that end in:

-ción	la emoción (emotion)
-dad	la ciudad (city)
-ie	la especie (kind, sort)
-umbre	la muchedumbre (crowd)
-ud	la multitud (multitude)

The following endings generally indicate a masculine gender:

-e	el tanque (tank)
-l	el hotel (hotel)
-n	el boletín (bulletin)
-r	el terror (terror)
-s	(in the singular) el interés (interest)

¡OJO! There are exceptions which you will learn to recognize.

4-1 SUSTANTIVOS *(continued)*

PLURALS

Nouns that end in a consonant add "-es": el reloj (clock; watch), los relojes.

Nouns that end in a vowel, add "-s": la casa, las casas.

Nouns that end in "z," change the "z" to "c" before adding "-es": la luz (light), las luces.

S The articles in Spanish function as adjectives; therefore they must agree in number and gender with the noun they modify: el libro, los libros; la taza (cup), las tazas; un hombre, una mujer (a man or one man; a woman or one woman).

When the indefinite article is pluralized its meaning changes: unos hombres (some, a few men); unas mujeres (some, a few women).

POSSESSIVES

In Spanish there is no apostrophe "s" to indicate possession or ownership. "This is John's suit." becomes "Este es el vestido de Juan." "The girls' parents are here." becomes "Los padres de las muchachas están aquí."

ACCENT MARKS

Nouns ending in "-n" or "-s" with an accent mark in the last syllable in the singular generally drop the accent mark in the plural: la estación, las estaciones; el jardín, los jardines; el inglés (the Englishman), los ingleses. There are exceptions: el país, los países.

Nouns of more than one syllable ending in "n," with no accent mark over the last syllable, generally carry an accent mark in the plural form: el crimen (crime), los crímenes; la orden (order), las órdenes; el joven (the young man), los jóvenes.

DIMINUTIVES

Diminutives are noun (sometimes adjective) endings used to express size, indicating either an affectionate or derogatory meaning. Students should be aware of their existence but should not use them until they are well along in their study of the language. Be familiar with some of them for the sake of comprehension:

-ito/a; -cito/a: Indicate either smallness, affection, generally favorable: un librito (a little book); una sillita (a little chair); un hombrecito (a nice little man); una mujercita (a nice little woman)

© 1996 by the Center for Applied Research in Education

-illo/a; -cillo/a: un hombrecillo (a little, unimportant man); una mujercilla (a little woman); un chiquillo (a kid, boy); una chiquilla (a little girl)

AUGMENTATIVES

-ón; -ona: un hombrón (a big ["he"] man); una mujerona (a large woman)

-ote/a: un librote (a heavy book); una mujer grandota (a hulking woman)

-azo/a: un perrazo (a big [bad] dog), m.; una perraza, f.

-ucho/a - acho/a (always derogatory): una casucha (a hovel); un vinacho (a poor quality wine)

4-2 Diálogo: Una familia cariñosa

Traduzca usted: La familia López—padre, madre, hijo, hija—están comiendo una cena que la madre ha preparado con mucho cuidado porque es el día de cumpleaños de su marido.

Sra. López:	(a su esposo) Amorcito, ¿te gusta la comidita que he preparado especialmente para complacer a mi maridito?
Sr. López:	Pues, sí, mujercita, está muy rica. ¿Verdad, hijito, hijita?
Hijo:	¡Por supuesto, papacito! ¿Verdad, hermanita?
Hija:	¡Ya lo creo, hermanito! Gracias, mamacita.

¡Qué familia tan amable vive en esta casita!

Traduzca usted en inglés y subraye (subrayar = to underline) los diminutivos.

Note usted cómo el uso de diminutivos nos demuestra que los miembros de esta familia se quieren unos a otros.

Vocabulario

cariñosa (loving)

el día de cumpleaños (birthday)

complacer (to please)

muy rica (delicious)

amable (lovable)

nos demuestra [demostrar] (shows)

© 1996 by the Center for Applied Research in Education

4-3 ¿MASCULINO O FEMENINO?

A	C	C	I	D	E	N	T	E	T	A	B	M	O	C
U	N	A	M	I	Z	U	R	E	D	N	E	D	R	O
T	O	S	R	A	I	Z	I	M	E	T	R	E	U	S
O	Z	I	A	M	L	T	B	O	R	O	R	R	E	T
M	A	R	C	A	L	B	U	M	A	R	R	O	Z	U
O	R	I	E	N	T	E	N	E	J	A	S	N	E	M
V	E	G	E	T	A	L	A	P	O	E	L	I	A	B
I	M	A	G	E	N	I	L	O	I	V	I	G	O	R
L	E	N	G	U	A	J	E	S	I	S	A	F	N	E
T	S	O	Z	N	C	U	V	O	Z	E	B	U	U	T
E	T	I	N	E	E	G	U	A	N	T	E	R	N	R
T	O	S	E	M	I	U	L	D	U	A	H	O	O	O
N	W	I	V	I	T	E	E	D	I	M	A	R	I	P
A	A	V	E	R	E	T	G	Z	L	O	S	O	V	S
T	E	E	I	C	Y	E	N	I	A	T	E	T	A	N
S	B	L	N	O	R	T	A	P	Ñ	O	M	O	B	A
N	U	E	L	A	M	I	N	A	E	R	U	M	O	R
I	N	T	E	R	E	S	O	L	S	E	R	R	O	T

In the word square there are 52 nouns that do not end in either "o" or "a." Find them; circle them and list them next to the English equivalents. Include the definite articles.

© 1996 by the Center for Applied Research in Education

¿¿
MASCULINO
o
FEMENINO
??

4-3 ¿MASCULINO O FEMENINO? (continued)

1. accident _____
2. airplane _____
3. album _____
4. angel _____
5. animal _____
6. automobile _____
7. boss _____
8. cloud _____
9. combat _____
10. corn _____
11. cough _____
12. crime _____
13. custom _____
14. dance _____
15. diamond _____
16. emphasis _____
17. furor _____
18. glove _____
19. image _____
20. instant _____
21. interest _____
22. language _____
23. luck _____
24. message _____
25. month _____
26. motor _____

27. name _____
28. net _____
29. noise _____
30. oil _____
31. order _____
32. Orient _____
33. pencil _____
34. pyramid _____
35. reason _____
36. rice _____
37. root _____
38. sea _____
39. sign _____
40. snow _____
41. sun _____
42. television _____
43. terror _____
44. tomato _____
45. tower _____
46. toy _____
47. transportation _____
48. tribunal _____
49. vegetable _____
50 vigor _____
51. violin _____
52. voice _____

4-4 TRES COSAS

(a) En el primer espacio escriba el número; (b) en el segundo espacio escriba el artículo definido del sustantivo dado; y (c) escriba una frase.

uno _____ **(1) El accidente fue terrible.** _____

_____ (3) _____ acordeón _____

_____ (5) _____ actitud _____

_____ (7) _____ actriz _____

_____ (9) _____ alcohol _____

_____ (11) _____ algodón _____

_____ (13) _____ arroz _____

_____ (15) _____ balcón _____

_____ (17) _____ botón _____

_____ (19) _____ calle _____

_____ (21) _____ canción _____

_____ (23) _____ cheque _____

_____ (25) _____ colección _____

_____ (27) _____ crimen _____

_____ (29) _____ deporte _____

_____ (31) _____ detalle _____

_____ (33) _____ edad _____

_____ (35) _____ examen _____

_____ (37) _____ flor _____

_____ (39) _____ frente _____

_____ (41) _____ frase _____

_____ (43) _____ gente _____

_____ (45) _____ habitación _____

_____ (47) _____ honor _____

4-4 TRES COSAS (continued)

_____ (49) __ hotel _____

_____ (51) __ interés _____

_____ (53) __ jardín _____

_____ (55) __ lápiz _____

_____ (57) __ libertad _____

_____ (59) __ limón _____

_____ (61) __ maíz _____

_____ (63) __ mar _____

_____ (65) __ motor _____

_____ (67) __ nación _____

_____ (69) __ nieve _____

_____ (71) __ origen _____

_____ (73) __ opinión _____

_____ (75) __ país _____

_____ (77) __ pan _____

_____ (79) __ papel _____

_____ (81) __ parte _____

_____ (83) __ plan _____

_____ (85) __ profesión _____

_____ (87) __ protección _____

_____ (89) __ región _____

_____ (91) __ salud _____

_____ (93) __ sed _____

_____ (95) __ tarde _____

_____ (97) __ tenis _____

_____ (99) __ uniforme _____

_____ (101) __ voz _____

© 1996 by the Center for Applied Research in Education

4-5 NÚMEROS: UNAS INDICACIONES MÁS

The word "y" (and) is not used after "ciento."

El vestido cuesta ciento cincuenta dólares ($150).

Numbers above one thousand are always expressed with "mil."

Yo nací en mil novecientos treinta y uno (1931).

Periods, not commas, are used to mark off thousands in Spanish.*

Una tonelada (ton) consta de 2.000 libras (2,000).

The hundreds from 2 to 900 have masculine and feminine forms. They agree with the noun they modify.

doscient<u>os</u> libr<u>os</u>
doscient<u>as</u> escuel<u>as</u>

"Un millón" is followed by "de" before nouns.

El señor Fulano tiene más de un millón <u>de</u> dólares.

¡DISCÚTANLO!

¿Se puede determinar el número de gotas de agua (raindrops) que cae en un determinado espacio? ¿Cómo?

Deletree usted (spell) el número dado.

1. 16 _____ alumnos

2. 101 _____ voces

3. 200 _____ mujeres

4. 1,000,000 _____ años

5. 21 _____ lápices

6. 1996 _____

7. $5.35 _____

8. 100 _____ películas

9. 102 _____ estudiantes

10. 300 _____ soldados

*Some Latin American countries have adopted the use of the comma.

4-5 NÚMEROS: UNAS INDICACIONES MÁS *(continued)*

CLASS ACTIVITY

Within groups or with a partner, ask questions involving numbers. Here are some examples:

¿Cuál es tu número de teléfono?

¿Cuánto dinero tienes en la bolsa?

¿En qué año naciste?

¿Cuántos años tienes?

© 1996 by the Center for Applied Research in Education

4-6 READ THE STAR

With a straight line connect the angles. Work clockwise. Write the numbers given, in figures. At the bottom of the page spell out the current year. Please notice the footnotes.

DOSCIENTOS

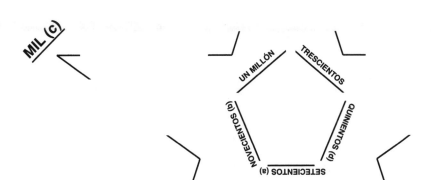

MIL (c)

CUATROCIENTOS

UN MILLÓN

TRESCIENTOS

NOVECIENTOS (b)

QUINIENTOS (d)

SETECIENTOS (a)

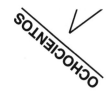

OCHOCIENTOS

SEISCIENTOS

Estamos en el año _____

(a) "sete-", NOT "siete-"
(b) "nove-", NOT "nueve-"
(c) NOT preceded by "un"
(d) "quinientos" NOT "cincocientos"

SYNONYMS AND ANTONYMS

SINÓNIMOS

Y

ANTÓNIMOS

5-1 ¡BUSQUE EL SINÓNIMO!

Sinónimos son dos palabras (a veces más) con la misma—o muy parecida—significación.

En la segunda columna subraye usted el sinónimo del verbo de la primera columna. En la tercera columna dé usted el significado en inglés, según el ejemplo:

VERBO	SINÓNIMO	
1. acabar	**<u>terminar</u>, empezar, arreglar**	to end _____
2. andar	parar, caminar, culminar	_____
3. atravesar	cruzar, tachar, contrariar	_____
4. conducir	convivir, condenar, guiar	_____
5. comprender	robar, entender, comprometer	_____
6. contestar	comparar, resistir, responder	_____
7. colocar	poner, colorar, columpiar	_____
8. enviar	mandar, escapar, aliviar	_____
9. reunir	reír, juntar, comparar	_____
10. suceder	convidar, suicidarse, ocurrir	_____

WHAT ARE THEY?

(a) Write down the first letter of each synonym in the second column above. (b) From these letters you can spell three 5-letter verbs. What are they? _____.
(c) Give synonyms of those three verbs _____.

THE RIGHT VERB

Complete the following sentences with the appropriate verb selected from the "verbo" list, 1-10 above.

1. Hasta hoy no se sabe qué va a _____ mañana.

2. El quinceañero (15-year-old) no puede_____el coche de su padre.

3. Al _____ el año escolar, los estudiantes quieren irse de vacaciones.

4. Quiero_____ una carta a mis tíos en Ecuador.

5. "La cucaracha, la cucaracha, ya no puede_____ porque le falta, porque no tiene gasolina con que _____." (This little ditty was popular during the Mexican Revolution. It refers to Pancho Villa's dilapidated automobile that constantly stalled.)

5-2 MATCH ME WITH ANOTHER ADJECTIVE IN ENGLISH

Remember that a synonym must be the same part of speech as its mate.

1. **aplicado**	<u>diligente</u>, chistoso, amargo	<u>diligent</u> _____
2. bastante	blando, severo, suficiente	_____
3. célebre	famoso, célibe, contento	_____
4. delgado	definido, cumplido, flaco	_____
5. grave	serio, enterrado, malvado	_____
6. hábil	proficiente, estudioso, serio	_____
7. indiferente	cuidadoso, descuidado, turbado	_____
8. ingenioso	creativo, laborioso, chistoso	_____
9. navegable	dirigible, inmóvil, llano	_____
10. obstinado	tenaz, blando, simple	_____

© 1996 by the Center for Applied Research in Education

5-3 DESCRIBE ME

Complete usted las frases siguientes con el adjetivo apropiado.

1. El indio de Guatemala es muy_____en los tejidos (weaving) a mano.

2. Hernán Cortés es el más_____de los conquistadores.

3. La obra del artista mexicano Diego Rivera es_____.

4. Don Quijote es un hombre alto y_____.

5. El burro es un animal_____.

6. El Prado en Madrid es un museo_____.

7. El Río Guadalquivir es el más_____ de España.

5-4 FIND MY NOUN MATE

Underline the noun synonym in column 2; give the English equivalent in the third column.

1.	**la alcoba**	**el dormitorio**, la sala, el baño	bedroom _____
2.	el amo	el padre, el novio, el dueño	_____
3.	el automóvil	el andén, el coche, la dirección	_____
4.	el cabello	la verdura, el cable, el pelo	_____
5.	la cárcel	la carne, el auto, la prisión	_____
6.	el cura	la curación, el sacerdote, la cara	_____
7.	la dama	la señora, el juego, la prensa	_____
8.	el edificio	la oficina, el inmueble, la escuela	_____
9.	el idioma	el dios, la palabra, la lengua	_____
10.	el lugar	el sitio, el animal, el hogar	_____

MYSTERY NOUN

Write the first letter of each noun in the first column above. _____
Some of the letters will spell a noun that means "concept." What is it? _____

© 1996 by the Center for Applied Research in Education

5-5 THE RIGHT NOUN, PLEASE

En el espacio escriba usted el sustantivo apropiado.

1. El_____ de Pedro es nuevo.

2. La reina de Inglaterra es una gran_____.

3. En España el_____ se llama_____; en México se llama "recámara."

4. El_____ de la casa vive en el primer piso (first floor).

5. La_____ no es un_____ deseable.

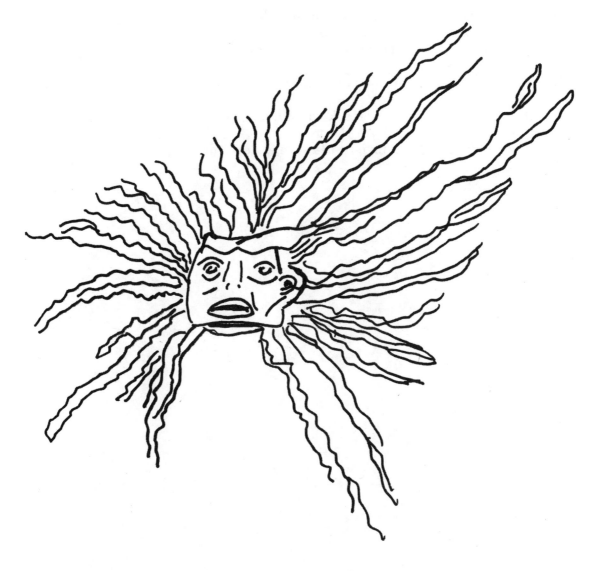

5-6 SUSTANTIVOS OPUESTOS

Antónimos son palabras que expresan ideas opuestas o contrarias.

En la segunda columna subraye usted la palabra de significación opuesta a la palabra en la primera columna. En la tercera columna dé usted la significación en inglés de las dos palabras, según el ejemplo dado.

1. **el amigo**	**el amo, el amparo, <u>el enemigo</u>**	**friend—enemy**
2. el amor	el olor, el odio, el afecto	_____
3. la dama	el drama, el niño, el caballero	_____
4. el norte	el sur, el oeste, el este	_____
5. la paz	el pedazo, la guerra, el puño	_____
6. la entrada	la ensalada, la sala, la salida	_____
7. el frío	el calor, el feo, el frontón	_____
8. el éxito	la entrada, el fracaso, el pasado	_____
9. la muerte	la suerte, la mordida, la vida	_____
10. el verano	el invierno, la verdad, la verdura	_____

5-7 MYSTERY NOUNS

En las frases siguientes escriba usted las palabras antónimas en los espacios. (A hint) La primera letra de cada palabra está dada.

1. El e __ __ __ __ es preferible al f __ __ __ __ __ __ __.

2. La m __ __ __ __ __ es el fin de la v __ __ __.

3. En el i __ __ __ __ __ __ __ __ hace f __ __ __; en el v __ __ __ __ __ __ hace c __ __ __ __.

4. En la Guerra Civil de los Estados Unidos el n __ __ __ __ luchó contra el s __ __.

5. En el teatro se paga a la e __ __ __ __ __ __ __ y no a la s __ __ __ __ __ __.

6. El a __ __ __ y el o __ __ __ no pueden convivir.

7. La g __ __ __ __ __ es destructiva; la p __ __ es constructiva.

8. El c __ __ __ __ __ __ __ __ __ andante siempre tiene una d __ __ __ __ a quien dedicar sus hazañas (deeds).

9. Un a __ __ __ __ es preferible a un e __ __ __ __ __ __ __.

10. Cuando hace f __ __ __ se puede esquiar; cuando hace c __ __ __ __ se puede nadar.

5-8 VERB ANTONYMS

In the second column underline the antonym of the verb in the first column. In the third column give the English translation of both verbs, as in the example given.

1. **abrir**	callar, <u>cerrar</u>, sentir	<u>open - close</u>
2. aparecer	perder, dormir, desaparecer	_____
3. callar	hablar, comer, punir	_____
4. contestar	comprar, preguntar, caminar	_____
5. encender	oler, entrar, apagar	_____
6. jugar	romper, trabajar, pagar	_____
7. perder	lograr, poder, ganar	_____
8. recordar	bailar, olvidar, caminar	_____
9. salir	comer, entrar, reír	_____
10. subir	pedir, leer, bajar	_____

- -

5-9 CLASS CONTEST

Have a class contest. Using the above verbs, plus a few others listed below, one student, or the teacher, will call out the verb; whoever thinks of its antonym first calls it out.

<u>ADDITIONAL ANTONYMS</u>

amar (odiar)	levantarse (acostarse, sentarse)
comprar (vender)	llorar (reír)
divertirse (aburrirse)	dar (recibir)
permitir (prohibir)	empezar (terminar)
ponerse (quitarse)	ensuciar (limpiar)
morir (vivir)	correr (caminar)

© 1996 by the Center for Applied Research in Education

5-10 Adjective Antonyms

In the second column underline the antonym. In the third column give the English equivalent of both Spanish adjectives, as in the example given.

1. alto	**alerta, <u>bajo</u>, gordo**	**tall - short**
2. ausente	austero, claro, presente	_____
3. blando	duro, prieto, duradero	_____
4. bueno	capaz, bonito, malo	_____
5. corto	largo, curioso, cálido	_____
6. difícil	diferente, fácil, durable	_____
7. grande	pequeño, gordo, rico	_____
8. mejor	malo, peor, pequeño	_____
9. mismo	sucio, salado, diferente	_____
10. obscuro	claro, obstinado, enfermo	_____

5-11 TELL ME THE TRUTH, PLEASE
(A/B Teacher Page)

Going up and down each row, one student will make a statement, such as, "Yo soy alto." The next student will answer negatively, "No, tú eres <u>bajo</u>," etc. Following is a list of additional adjective antonyms. If a student comes up with an adjective not on the lists, better still! It will be a challenge to the one who has to answer.

ADDITIONAL ADJECTIVE ANTONYMS

alegre	triste	hermoso	feo
amargo	dulce	inteligente	estúpido
ancho	estrecho	ligero	pesado
antiguo	moderno	limpio	sucio
barato	caro	lleno	vacío
blanco	negro	mayor	menor
bueno	malo	mucho	poco
común	raro	primero	último
débil	fuerte	rubio	moreno
este	oeste	valiente	cobarde
		vivo	muerto

Section 6

PREFIJOS Y SUFIJOS
(PREFIXES AND SUFFIXES)

PREFIJOS Y SUFIJOS

6-1 PREFIXES (Vocabulary)

El prefijo es <u>ante</u>puesto a una palabra. Usualmente aclara la significación de la palabra. Por ejemplo, "pre-" (before) "-fijo" (fixed). Familiaridad con prefijos y sufijos ayuda a aumentar su vocabulario. Las palabras son esenciales en la comunicación. Si usted comprende una palabra clave en una conversación o en un mensaje escrito, usted puede comprender la esencia del mensaje.

Hágase amigo con este grupo de prefijos:

a-; an- (negation) <u>a</u>normal (abnormal)

anfi- (around) <u>anfi</u>teatro (amphitheatre)

ante- (before) <u>ante</u>ayer (day before yesterday)

anti- (in opposition) <u>anti</u>ácido (antacid)

bi-; bis- (twice; double) <u>bi</u>cicleta (bicycle); <u>bis</u>abuelo (great-grandfather)

circu- (around) <u>circu</u>nferencia (circumference)

co-; con- (together) <u>co</u>laborar (collaborate; work together); <u>con</u>dominio (condominium; joint ownership)

contra- (opposition to) <u>contra</u>veneno (antidote; counter poison)

de-; des- (without; separation) <u>de</u>generar (degenerate); <u>des</u>esperar (despair; lose hope)

di-; dis- (to separate; to deprive) <u>di</u>slocar (dislocate); <u>di</u>cotomía (dichotomy; division into two parts)

en- (place in which; acquisition of a quality); <u>en</u>jaular (to place in a cage); <u>en</u>flaquecer (to become thin)

entre- (between) <u>entre</u>acto (intermission)

epi- (outer, over) <u>epi</u>dermis (epidermis; over the skin)

ex- (outside; direction toward) <u>ex</u>portar (to export)

hemi- (half) <u>hemi</u>sferio (hemisphere)

hiper- (excess) <u>hi</u>pertensión (hypertension)

hipo- (under) <u>hipo</u>dérmica (hypodermic; under the skin)

i-; in- (negation) <u>i</u>legal (illegal); <u>in</u>moral (immoral)

inter- (between) <u>inter</u>nacional (international)

intra- (inside) <u>intra</u>venosa (intravenous)

macro- (large) <u>macro</u>cosmo (macrocosm; large universe)

micro- (small) <u>micro</u>scopio (microscope)

para- (along with) <u>para</u>militar (paramilitary)

pos-; post- (afterwards) <u>pos</u>poner (postpone); <u>post</u>graduado/a (postgraduate)

6-1 PREFIXES (Vocabulary) (continued)

pro- (forward) <u>pro</u>greso (progress)

re- (repetition; step backwards) <u>re</u>accionar (to react)

sobre- (superiority; excess) <u>sobre</u>humano (superhuman)

super- (above) <u>super</u>poner (superimpose)

so-; sub- (underneath) <u>so</u>cavar (to dig under, undermine); <u>sub</u>terráneo (underground)

tele- (distant) <u>tele</u>scopio (telescope)

tras-; trans (beyond; across) <u>tras</u>ladar (to transfer); <u>trans</u>parente (transparent)

tri- (three) <u>tri</u>mestre (trimester)

ultra- (beyond) <u>ultra</u>liberal (ultraliberal)

vi-; vice-; viz- (instead of; in place of); <u>vi</u>cario (vicar; a person who acts in place of another); <u>vice</u>presidente (vice president); <u>viz</u>conde (viscount—pronounced vī´-kount)

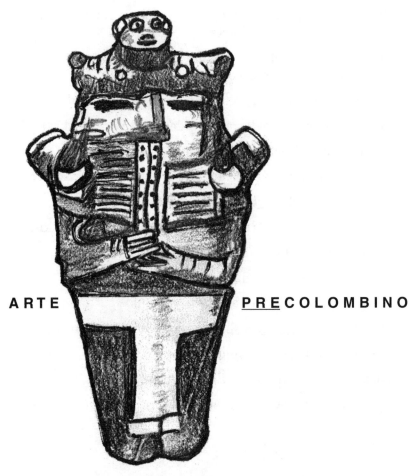

ARTE **<u>PRE</u>COLOMBINO**

(pre-Columbian art)

90

© 1996 by the Center for Applied Research in Education

6-2 COMPLETE THE WORDS

Complete usted las palabras en los espacios.

Ejemplo: El niño maneja su bi <u>cicleta</u> muy bien.

1. Yo vivo con mis padres en un con_____.

2. Un sabio (wise man) puede pre_____una catástrofe.

3. Con un tele_____ se puede ver la Vía Láctea (Milky Way).

4. Conducir un coche sin una póliza de seguros es i_____.

5. Los griegos (Greeks) construyeron muchos anfi_____.

6. Ante_____ pasamos el día en el Parque Central.

7. Jugando al béisbol, Juan se dis_____el codo.

8. Cien días sin lluvia es a_____.

9. El arquitecto y el constructor co_____ en la construcción de un edificio.

10. El pre_____ es la primera parte de una palabra.

11. Cuando llueve, esta calle es intrans_____.

12. Un micro_____ se usa para ver objetos pequeños.

13. Un proseta es una persona que no puede pro_____.

14. El problema es super_____.

15. Con un tele_____se puede ver a larga distancia.

6-3 LOOK-ALIKES BUT DIFFERENT

Explique usted la diferencia ente los prefijos siguientes. Uselos en una palabra. Los primeros dos están hechos.

Ejemplo:

1. ante- (before) antepagar (prepay)

2. anti- (in opposition) anticuerpo (antibody)

3. con-

4. contra-

5. inter-

6. intra-

7. macro-

8. micro-

9. pre-

10. pro-

11. hiper-

12. hipo-

© 1996 by the Center for Applied Research in Education

6-4 SUFFIXES (Vocabulary)

El sufijo es pospuesto a una palabra. Algunos tienen un significado especial:

-algia (pain) neur<u>algia</u> (neuralgia; pain in a nerve)

-cida (which kills) homi<u>cida</u> (homicide, manslaughter)

-ciclo (wheel) tri<u>ciclo</u> (tricycle; 3 wheels)

-cracia (power) demo<u>cracia</u> (democracy; government by the people)

-cultor (which cultivates) agri<u>cultor</u> (agricultural; connected with farming)

-fobia (fear) claustro<u>fobia</u> (claustrophobia; fear of confined space)

-fugo/a (escape) centrí<u>fugo</u> (centrifugal; moving away from the center)

-grafo (which writes) telé<u>grafo</u> (telegraph; distance writing)

-itis (inflammation) tonsil<u>itis</u> (tonsillitis; inflammation of the tonsils)

-logía; -logo (science) bio<u>logía</u> (biology; study of animal and plant life);
    astró<u>logo</u> (astrologer; one who studies the stars)

Hay otros sufijos que tienen una equivalencia en inglés. Por ejemplo, muchas palabras que terminan en "-tad" o "-dad" en español terminan en "-ty" en inglés:

anormalidad	abnormality
calidad	quality
cantidad	quantity
deformidad	deformity
dificultad	difficulty
facultad	faculty
flexibilidad	flexibility
inmunidad	immunity
maternidad	maternity
nacionalidad	nationality
necesidad	necessity
oportunidad	opportunity
posibilidad	possibility
regularidad	regularity

Hay otros sufijos que tienen una semejanza en las dos lenguas:

-acio	prefacio	preface
-ador	senador	senator
-aje	follaje	foliage
-al	pedestal	pedestal
-ante	dominante	dominant
-ble	honorable	honorable
-cial	potencial	potential
-ción	nación	nation
-encia	contingencia	contingency
-ente	continente	continent
-ica	música	music
-ión	comunión	communion
-ismo	alcoholismo	alcoholism
-ista	pianista	pianist
-ito	infinito	infinite
-ivo	agresivo	aggressive
-or	menor	minor
-oso	famoso	famous
-ura	conjetura	conjecture

© 1996 by the Center for Applied Research in Education

6-5 ¡JUGUEMOS "OLÉ"! (LET'S PLAY "OLÉ!")

Each student will select ten Spanish words from the list of "-tad" or "-dad" endings, writing each word on a separate slip of paper. He or she will then make an alphabetical list of the ENGLISH equivalents of those words on a sheet of paper which he will keep, giving the separate slips to the teacher. When all the slips have been collected, they will be put in a container and scrambled. The teacher will pick out one slip at a time, calling out the word it contains IN SPANISH. Whoever has its English equivalent will call it out and check it off his list. The first one who checks off the ten words will call out "Olé" and will win the prize—whatever it may be!

TRAMPAS (PITFALLS)

¡PASO A PASO, CON CUIDADO! (STEP BY STEP, WITH CARE!)

Chichen Itzá, México

7-1 PITFALLS (TRAMPAS) (Background)

Unless you are made aware of pitfalls–which every language has–you are likely to be tripped up. Here are a few.

¡OJO! "del" and "de él": "Del" is a contraction of two words, the preposition "de" (of) and the masculine definite article "el."

El repertorio del actor es sobresaliente.
(The actor's repertory is outstanding.)
El problema de él no es serio.
(His problem is not serious.)

You can say "Su problema . . ." but that would not be clear since it could mean "your problem," "his problem," "her problem," or "their problem."

¡OJO! In the combinations "gua" and "guo," the "u" is always pronounced as "w": agua, lengua, lenguón (S. A., talkative). When a "u" comes between an "e" or an "i" it sometimes carries a dieresis (¨) which indicates that the sound of the "u" as a "w" is maintained: bilingüe (bēē-lĭn-gwĕh, bilingual), cigüeña (sēē-gwĕn-ya, stork), as opposed to words like aguilón (ah-ghēē-lawn, large eagle), guisado (ghēē-sah-daw, stew), maguey (mah-gay, century plant). In these cases the "u" is silent and is there only to give the hard sound of the "g" which otherwise would be aspirated before an "i" or an "e": genial (hĕh-nēē-ahl, genial), gitano (hēē-tah-naw, gypsy).

¡OJO! Although the letter "h" is not sounded in Spanish it must not be omitted in spelling. Pronounce these words to enhance the ear sound and the eye image.

ahora	hasta
hablar	hombre
hambre	honor
hacienda	hostil
harina	humanidad

¡OJO! Nouns may be used as adjectives in English: a <u>brick</u> house, but NOT in Spanish: una casa <u>de ladrillos</u> (a house of bricks).

¡OJO! When two or more adverbs modify a verb, "-mente" (equivalent to "-ly" in English) is added only to the final adverb.

El presidente habló rápida, clara e inteligentemente.
(The president spoke rapidly, clearly, and intelligently.)

¡OJO! For ease in pronunciation the masculine definite article "el" is used before singular, feminine nouns beginning with a stressed "a" or "ha."

SINGULAR	PLURAL
el hacha (axe)	las hachas
el águila (eagle)	las águilas
el alma (soul)	las almas

This also applies to the indefinite article:

un águila	unas águilas
un alma	unas almas

¡OJO! Some words have the same spelling but different meanings when written with or without an accent.

él (pro.)◄───► el (def. art., masc. sing.)

> **Él es un gran hombre.**
> **(He is a great man.)**
> **El libro está en el suelo.**
> **(The book is on the floor.)**

┌─► mí (pro., obj. of prep.)

> **El regalo es para mí.**
> **(The gift is for me.)**

└─► mi (poss. pro.)

> **¿Te gusta mi vestido?**
> **(Do you like my dress?)**

┌─► sé (pres. tense of "saber"; "I know.")

> **Yo sé que él va a venir a la fiesta.**
> **(I know he is coming to the party.)**

└─► se (refl. pro.)

> **El niño se viste solo.**
> **(The child dresses by himself.)**

┌─► sólo (adv., only)

> **Sólo quería verlo una vez más.**
> **(I only wanted to see him once more.)**

└─► solo (adj., alone, lonely)

> **Carlos no tiene compañía; está solo.**
> **(Carlos does not have any company; he is alone.)**

┌─► té (n., tea)

> **Los ingleses toman té por la tarde.**
> **(The English people take tea in the afternoon.)**

└─► te (object. pro., you)

© 1996 by the Center for Applied Research in Education

7-1 PITFALLS (TRAMPAS) (Background) *(continued)*

Yo te quiero mucho.
(I love you very much.)

→ tú (nom. pro., you)

Tú eres el mejor estudiante de la clase.
(You are the best student in the class.)

→ tu (poss. adj.)

Tu padre es muy estricto.
(Your father is very strict.)

¡OJO! Palabras frecuentemente usadas incorrectamente.

→ aparecer (to appear, be seen)

Lo esperé por mucho tiempo, y de repente, apareció.
(I waited for him for a long time and suddenly, he appeared.)

→ parecer (to seem)

El payaso parecía triste.
(The clown seemed sad.)

→ campo (country, as opposed to the city)

Este año vamos a pasar las vacaciones en el campo.
(This year we are going to spend our vacation in the country.)

→ país (country, native land)

La Argentina es el país donde nació el famoso escritor, Jorge
Luis Borges.
(Argentina is the country where the famous writer, Jorge Luis
Borges, was born.)

→ carácter (personal traits)

Es un hombre de buen carácter.
(He is a man of good character.)

→ personaje (character in a play, book)

Don Quijote es un personaje universal.
(Don Quijote is a universal character.)

→ preguntar (to ask a question)

Ese hombre me preguntó dónde vive el presidente de los
Estados Unidos.
(That man asked me where the President of the United States
lives.)

→ pedir (to ask for something)

Los mendigos piden limosna.
(The beggars ask for alms.)

oír (to hear sound)

Siempre oigo ruidos extraños en la casa.
(I always hear strange sounds in the house.)

escuchar (to listen to)

Me gusta escuchar la radio.
(I like to listen to the radio.)

volver (to come back)

Él quiere volver a su país.
(He wants to return to his native country.)

devolver (to return something)

Tengo que devolver estos libros a la biblioteca.
(I have to return these books to the library.)

gastar (to spend money)

A Luis no le gusta gastar dinero.
(Louis does not like to spend money.)

pasar (to spend time)

José pasa mucho tiempo en la playa.
(Joseph spends a lot of time on the beach.)

sacar fotos (to take pictures)

A Juan le gusta sacar fotos de su familia.
(John likes to take photos of his family.)

dar un paseo (to take a walk)

Después de comer damos un paseo por la Alameda.
(After eating we take a walk along the Alameda.)

bajo (under, NOT underneath)

Cuba cambió mucho bajo el gobierno de Fidel Castro.
(Cuba changed a lot under Fidel Castro's government.)

debajo de (under, literally, buried)

El pobre perro está debajo del manzano.
(The poor dog is buried under the apple tree.)

¡OJO! To translate "in," "de" must follow a superlative in Spanish.

El Mississippi es el río más largo de los Estados Unidos.
(The Mississippi is the longest river in the United States.)

© 1996 by the Center for Applied Research in Education

7-1 PITFALLS (TRAMPAS) (Background) *(continued)*

¡OJO! One word or two?

→ porque (conj., because)

> **Clara no quiso venir a la fiesta porque no se sentía bien.**
> **(Clara did not want to come to the party because she was not feeling well.)**

→ por qué (adv., why?)

> **¿Por qué lo hiciste?**
> **(Why did you do it?)**

→ para qué (why? What is the aim?)

> **¿Para qué inventaron esta máquina?**
> **(Why did they invent this machine? for what reason?)**

Present participle (-ing)

Gerundio: add "-ando" to -ar verbs: cantar—cantando
add "-iendo" to -er and -ir verbs: comer—comiendo; vivir–viviendo

¡OJO! To form the progressive tenses:
(I am walking–estoy caminando) or

the past progressive tenses:
(I was walking–estaba caminando)

combine the present participle with the verb "estar";

NEVER "ser."

> **Juan está comiendo.**
> **(John is eating.)**
> **Elena estaba cantando.**
> **(Helen was singing.)**

¡OJO! The Spanish present participle may NOT be used as a noun or adjective, as it may in English.

> **Seeing (n.) is believing (n.)**
> **(Ver es creer.)**
> **My father says that studying is important.**
> **(Mi padre dice que el estudiar es importante. —NOT "estudiando.")**

© 1996 by the Center for Applied Research in Education

7-2 ¿DÓNDE ESTÁ?

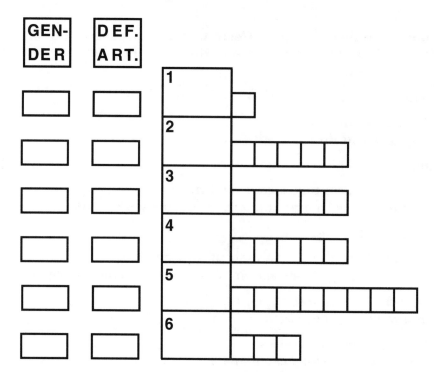

In the numbered boxes write the first letter of each word, which you will complete in the boxes that follow it to the right. They are words that are used in this section. Definitions are given below. Write the definite article that goes with each word and indicate whether it is masculine (m.), feminine (f.), or both (m., f.). If you fill in the proper words, the numbered squares will give you the name of something that you don't want to fall into. ¿Qué es?

1. something you drink

2. something you receive on your birthday

3. something that flies high

4. something that grows in the desert

5. someone in a book or play

6. something that sustains life

© 1996 by the Center for Applied Research in Education

7-3 ¡COMPLÉTEME!

Dé la palabra apropiada según el sentido de la frase.

1. El pirata tenía (an iron leg) _____.

2. El premio no es mío sino (his) _____.

3. (The eagle) _____ es (a bird) _____ de rapiña.

4. ¿Te gustó (my) _____ comida de anoche?

5. El político (only) _____ quería darle un beso al bebé.

6. El fantasma (appears) _____ (only) _____ (at night) _____.

7. (In the country) _____ hay muchos animales domésticos.

8. (I'm going to come back) _____ a las once de la noche.

9. Todos los (characters) _____ en el drama son interesantes.

10. No me gusta (to ask for) _____ favores.

11. Quiero (to take a walk) _____ por el Parque Central.

12. Manolo (knows) _____ la dirección de Lola.

Use words you supplied in sentences 3, 5, 6, and 7 to create a new sentence in the order given below. Then translate it into English.

3 _____

6 _____

7 _____

5 _____

6 _____

Spanish: _____

English: _____

© 1996 by the Center for Applied Research in Education

7-4 IDIOMS (Background/Vocabulary)

Idioms can also be pitfalls if you are not careful. An idiom is a peculiar phraseology that means something specific which cannot be expressed in any other way, least of all by word-for-word translation. There are many idioms in the Spanish language. Here are a few of the more useful ones.

acabar de (to have just + verb)

> **Acabo de leer el libro de García Márquez, "Cien años de soledad."**
> **(I have just read García Márquez' book, "One Hundred Years of Solitude.")**

a ver (Let's see.)

> **A ver cuánto dinero tienes.**
> **(Let's see how much money you have.)**

al pie de la letra (exactly)

> **El alcalde siguió la ley al pie de la letra.**
> **(The mayor followed the law exactly.)**

a propósito (by the way; on purpose)

> **A propósito, ¿quieres ir al cine conmigo?**
> **(By the way, do you want to go to the movies with me?)**
> **El muchacho rompió la ventana a propósito.**
> **(The boy broke the window on purpose.)**

a eso de (at about)

> **Anoche llegué a casa a eso de las once.**
> **(Last night I arrived home at about eleven.)**

a pesar de (in spite of)

> **A pesar de todo, Romeo y Julieta se amaron.**
> **(In spite of everything, Romeo and Juliet loved each other.)**

a lo lejos (in the distance)

> **A lo lejos se ven las montañas.**
> **(In the distance one can see the mountains.)**

boca abajo (face down)

> **El bebé duerme boca abajo.**
> **(The baby sleeps face down.)**

boca arriba (face up)

> **El herido estaba en el suelo, boca arriba.**
> **(The wounded man was on the ground, face up.)**

cuanto antes (as soon as possible)

> **Los estudiantes quieren ir de vacaciones cuanto antes.**
> **(The students want to go on vacation as soon as possible.)**

darse cuenta de (to become aware of, to realize)

> **Finalmente, se dio cuenta de su error.**
> **(Finally, he became aware of his error.)**

© 1996 by the Center for Applied Research in Education

© 1996 by the Center for Applied Research in Education

dar las gracias (to thank)

El niño les da las gracias a sus padres por los regalos de Navidad.
(The boy thanks his parents for his Christmas gifts.)

dar un paseo (to take a walk)

Después de comer doy un paseo por el parque.
(After eating I take a walk in the park.)

de repente (suddenly)

De repente, el bebé empezó a llorar.
(Suddenly, the baby started to cry.)

en voz alta (aloud, in a loud voice)

Los alumnos leen los poemas en voz alta.
(The pupils read the poems aloud.)

ir de compras (to go shopping)

La criada va de compras todos los días.
(The maid goes shopping every day.)

pedir perdón (to apologize)

Mi socio me pidió perdón por haber llegado tarde.
(My associate apologized for having arrived late.)

Lo siento mucho. (I am very sorry.)

soñar con (to dream about)

Anoche soñé contigo.
(Last night I dreamed of you.)

tomar el pelo (to tease)

Me estás tomando el pelo, ¿verdad?
(You're teasing me, aren't you?)

¿Qué pasa? (What's happening?)

¡Qué mala suerte! (What bad luck!)

¡Qué raro! (How strange!)

¡Qué divertido! (What fun! How amusing!)

¿Qué tal? (What's new? How are things?)

7-5 ¿CÓMO SE DICE? (DIÁLOGO)

Dos amigos se encuentran en la calle.

Miguel: (What's new?) _____, Carlos?
Carlos: Pues, nada en particular. Me siento un poco cansado.
Miguel: ¿Cansado? ¿Por qué?
Carlos: Pues, anoche (at about) _____ las once me acosté. Estaba leyendo "El Cid Campeador" en cama, cuando alguien tocó a la puerta. (How strange!) _____ pensé. ¿Quién será a esta hora? (In a loud voice) _____ pregunté, "¿Quién es?" "Soy yo, Alberto," respondió la voz. (I became aware) _____ de que era mi nuevo vecino. En la obscuridad no vio el número de la puerta y se había equivocado. (He apologized) _____ y se fue. Yo seguí leyendo "El Cid," y luego me quedé dormido (face up) _____, y (I dreamed of) _____ mi héroe, el Campeador, siguiéndole a caballo toda la noche.

VOCABULARIO

anoche (last night)

tocó a la puerta (knocked at the door)

¿Quién será? (Who can it be?)

vecino (neighbor)

la obscuridad (darkness)

Yo seguí leyendo. (I continued reading.)

siguiéndole a caballo (following him on horseback)

REFRANES (PROVERBS)

Abra
usted
la puerta
a la

sabiduría
antigua

8-1 REFRANES (Background)

Read REFRANES in Spanish. See how much you can understand. Then read the English translation on the following page.

Un refrán expresa una verdad básica o una experiencia común. A veces puede ser un enigma que contiene una verdad profunda.

Refranes son universales. Han sido escritos desde hace muchísimo tiempo. Por ejemplo, los egipcios antiguos decían que las peores situaciones del hombre son: estar en la cama y no dormir; anhelar (yearn) por alguien que no viene; tratar de agradar (to please) y no llegar a agradar. Éstas son verdades perpetuas.

El Rey Salomón de Israel en el siglo 10 a. de J.C. (B.C.) después de muchos años de vida activa, escribió "El libro de proverbios" con otros sabios (sages); contiene más de tres mil proverbios.

Los hombres de diferentes épocas pueden tener culturas variadas, y pueden ser distintos en otras facetas de la vida pero no cambian mucho en características básicas; así que un proverbio antiguo puede ser aplicable a un hombre de cualquier época, incluso al hombre moderno.

8-2 PROVERBS

A proverb expresses a basic truth or a common experience. It can sometimes be an enigma which contains a profound truth.

Proverbs are universal. They have been written since way back in time. For example, the ancient Egyptians used to say that the worst situations a man can experience are: to be in bed and not be able to sleep; to yearn for someone who does not come; to try to please, but fail to do so. These are perpetual truths.

King Solomon of Israel (10 B.C.) after many years of active living, wrote THE BOOK OF PROVERBS, with other wise men contributing. It contains more than three thousand proverbs.

Men of different epochs may have different cultures and can differ in other facets of life, but they do not change much in basic characteristics; so an ancient proverb may apply to a man of any era, including modern man.

8-3 Refranes de sabiduría

Traduzca usted al inglés los refranes siguientes:

1. Se aprende con la práctica.

   _____

2. El sol sale para todos.

   _____

3. Más vale tarde que nunca.

   _____

4. Una mano lava la otra.

   _____

5. Él que no trabaja, no come.

   _____

6. Mirar antes de saltar (leap).

   _____

7. Vivir y dejar vivir.

   _____

8. No todo lo que reluce (shines) es oro.

   _____

9. No dormirse sobre sus laureles (laurels).

   _____

10. Dime con quiénes andas, y te diré quién eres.

    _____

11. La curiosidad mató al gato.

    _____

 12. Después de la lluvia sale el sol.

    _____

© 1996 by the Center for Applied Research in Education

8-4 ¡Busque usted mi otra parte!

Unscramble the following proverbs. The first part of each statement is in the left-hand column; the second part is somewhere in the right-hand column. Find the proper second half and place its number next to its first half; then, on another sheet write out each proverb in Spanish with your version in English.

Example:

1. **En boca cerrada** _6_

2. Los pájaros de la misma pluma _____

3. No dejes para mañana _____

4. A quien madruga (gets up early) _____

5. Más vale pájaro en mano _____

6. Perro que ladra (barks) _____

7. Quien siembra (plants) vientos _____

8. Ojos que no ven _____

9. A caballo regalado _____

10. A buen entendedor _____

11. Haz lo que digo; _____

(1) corazón que no siente.

(2) recoje tempestades.

(3) vuelan juntos.

(4) lo que puedes hacer hoy.

(5) no se le mira el colmillo (eyetooth).

(6) no entran moscas.

(7) no muerde.

(8) Dios le ayuda.

(9) pocas palabras.

(10) que cien volando.

(11) no hagas lo que hago.

© 1996 by the Center for Applied Research in Education

8-5 SABIDURÍA EN INGLÉS Y EN ESPAÑOL
(Teacher's Page)

Dictate the proverbs on this page. If you give the Spanish version, the students will write the English meaning (or vice versa) on the student handout page that follows the proverbs.

1. En boca cerrada no entran moscas.
   (Silence is golden.)

2. Los pájaros de la misma pluma vuelan juntos.
   (Birds of a feather flock together.)

3. No dejes para mañana lo que puedes hacer hoy.
   (Don't leave for tomorrow what you can do today.)

4. A quien madruga Dios le ayuda.
   (The early bird catches the worm.)

5. Más vale pájaro en mano que cien volando.
   (A bird in the hand is worth two in the bush.)

6. Perro que ladra no muerde.
   (A barking dog does not bite.)

7. Quien siembra vientos recoje tempestades.
   (You reap what you sow.)

8. Ojos que no ven, corazón que no siente.
   (Out of sight, out of mind.)

9. A caballo regalado no se le miran los dientes.
   (Do not look a gift horse in the mouth.)

10. A buen entendedor pocas palabras.
    (A word to the wise is sufficient.)

11. ¡Haz lo que digo; no hagas lo que hago!
    (Do what I say; do not do what I do.)

8-5 Sabiduría en Inglés y en Español

1. Spanish: _____

   English: _____

2. Spanish: _____

   English: _____

3. Spanish: _____

   English: _____

4. Spanish: _____

   English: _____

5. Spanish: _____

   English: _____

6. Spanish: _____

   English: _____

7. Spanish: _____

   English: _____

8. Spanish: _____

   English: _____

9. Spanish: _____

   English: _____

10. Spanish: _____

    English: _____

11. Spanish: _____

    English: _____

12. Spanish: _____

    English: _____

Debemos comer para vivir,
no vivir para comer.

Molière (1622–1673)

9-1 AMOR Y CALORÍAS

Alicia: ¿Te gusta cocinar, María?

María: ¡Por supuesto! A mi novio le encantan mis recetas. Su plato favorito es arroz con pollo. Sabes, yo creo que el amor entra por la cocina.

Alicia: Tienes razón. Roberto te adora. Pero, dime, tú eres tan delgada; ¿cuentas las calorías de tus comidas?

María: Claro que las cuento. Quiero mantener la línea.

Alicia: Dichosa tú. Yo quiero perder peso, ¡pero es tan difícil hacerlo!

María: Pues, puede ser. Mi mamá me dice que para perder, o ganar, peso, se debe mantener un estricto control de las calorías de cada comida, pero sin pasar por alto los alimentos que conservan la salud, como las proteínas para ayudar a combatir las infecciones; el calcio para mantener fuertes los huesos y los dientes; el hierro para producir hemoglobina que lleva oxígeno a las células; los carbohidratos para dar energía al cuerpo; y sin olvidar las vitaminas "A" para mantener la vista, "D" para el buen desarrollo de los huesos, "C" para combatir las infecciones.

Alicia: ¡Uf! Suena muy complicado todo eso.

María: Verdaderamente, no lo es.

Alicia: Y nosotros que somos de sobrepeso, ¿qué más tenemos que hacer para adelgazar?

María: Pues, los ejercicios diarios también son importantes para mantener la salud y controlar el peso. Y ¡cuidado con los dulces!

Alicia: Eso, sí que es difícil para mí; me encantan tanto los dulces de chocolate.

María: Hay más: Las bebidas alcohólicas, las drogas y los cigarrillos son tabú. Mi novio, Roberto, y yo estamos de acuerdo en todo esto; así, gozamos de la vida.

Alicia: Cuando se casen, ¿quién va a cocinar?

María: ¡Él, por supuesto!

Alicia: Me parece muy bien. ¡Enhorabuena!

María: Ah, otra cosa, Alicia. Es muy importante consultar a un médico antes de someterte a un régimen alimenticio.

Alicia: Sí, voy a hacerlo. Tengo que perder peso. Quiero lucir como las modelos en la televisión.

VOCABULARIO

adelgazar (to become slender)

buen desarrollo (proper development)

enhorabuena (good luck!)

estamos de acuerdo (we agree)

lucir (to look like)

mantener la línea (to keep shapely)

no lo es (it is not)

pasar por alto (to overlook)

perder peso (to lose weight)

por supuesto (of course)

un régimen alimenticio (a diet)

9-2 "CIERTO" ES MÁS FÁCIL QUE "FALSO"

Read the dialogue, *Amor y Calorías,* 9-1. Mark each sentence "cierto" or "falso." If "falso," give the correct information.

1. Según María, el amor entra por la ventana. _____

_____

2. A María le gusta cocinar. _____

_____

3. El plato favorito del novio de María es salmón ahumado. _____

_____

4. Alicia está descontenta porque está gorda. _____

_____

5. María no sabe nada de calorías. _____

_____

6. El hierro produce debilidad en el cuerpo. _____

_____

7. Los carbohidratos dan energía al cuerpo. _____

_____

8. María y su novio no se entienden bien. _____

_____

9. Cuando María y Roberto se casen, María va a cocinar. _____

_____

10. Para María y Roberto la salud es secundaria. _____

_____

11. Alicia quiere lucir como las estrellas del cine. _____

_____

9-3 DIÁLOGO: EL HAMBRE ES LA MEJOR SALSA (A)

Es sábado, las once de la mañana. Elena y su hermano, Alfredo, le preguntan a su madre qué van a comer a mediodía.

Elena:	Mamá, tenemos hambre. ¿Qué vas a preparar para el almuerzo?
Mamá:	Pues, ¿tienen mucha hambre?
Elena:	Sí, mamá, no he comido nada desde anoche.
Alfredo:	¡Estoy hambriento!
Mamá:	Bien, entonces voy a preparar una tortilla de huevos y vegetales con un buen plato de arroz, y frijoles refritos.
Elena:	Eso suena muy bien, mamá—y ¿de postre?
Mamá:	De postre—flan y pastelitos.
Elena:	Te ayudo.
Alfredo:	Sí, sí, ¡Date prisa! A la una tengo que jugar al fútbol con mis amigos. Es un partido muy importante.
Elena:	Siempre tienes prisa. ¿Por qué no nos ayudas?

VOCABULARIO

pues (well)

mediodía (noontime)

hambre; tener hambre (to be hungry); tener mucha hambre (to be very hungry)

hambriento (a) (famished)

flan (custard)

anoche (last night)

tortilla (In Spain it is an omelet; in Mexico it is a flat pancake made of corn flour and eaten as bread with meals.)

el almuerzo (lunch)

el postre (dessert)

un partido (a game)

¡Date prisa! (Hurry!)

9-4 ¡SEA HONESTO/A!

Dé una respuesta honesta (en español) a las preguntas que siguen.

1. ¿Se lleva bien (llevarse bien = to get along with) con sus hermanos (sisters and brothers)?

   _____

   _____

2. Si no (if not), ¿por qué?

   _____

   _____

3. ¿Cuántos hermanos tiene usted? ¿Mayores or menores?

   _____

   _____

4. ¿Son rigurosos (strict) con usted sus padres?

   _____

   _____

5. ¿Sus padres son justos (fair) con usted?

   _____

   _____

6. ¿Cree usted que ser padres es fácil?

   _____

   _____

   En clase discutan problemas o lazos familiares (family problems or ties). (Traten de hacerlo en español.)

© 1996 by the Center for Applied Research in Education

9-5 Es verdad

Translate:

1. La obesidad es un estado mental que proviene del aburrimiento y la tristeza.

Cyril Connolly (1903–1974)

_____

_____

2. Dime lo que comes, y yo te diré lo que eres.

A. Brillat-Savarin (1755–1826)

_____

_____

3. No hay amor más sincero que el amor a la comida.

G. Bernard Shaw (1856–1950)

_____

_____

9-6 CONSEJO

In the word square find the equivalent, in Spanish, of the following statement: Eat, drink, and enjoy yourself, but tomorrow—DIET!

NOTE: The words can run from left to right or right to left, vertically, horizontally, or diagonally.

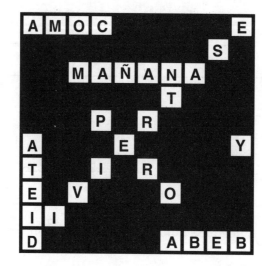

Give the three commands and their infinitives.

_____   _____

_____   _____

_____   _____

9-7 OUT OF ONE, MANY

```
P A R E D C P M R A X P O D E R
E A E M E R U U E P R A L L E A
R A R A R E R D M O W R A C O R
A O M E U E O O O R A D U M S O
O D U R C R S M C V I E O R E P
B L O E K E R C A R R O T S E A
E S P E R A R E S D F G C R I R
O R E C A D O M O P E R A R A C
C U E R O R C A D Q E L O E T O
O T R U E D A R A A L M K M R R
M S U C H U O X D R P O R O A A
P O M E R O D O A E R I D E N D
R I O R C A R M R C E R A A D O
A P R A R O E N T R A C E R O S
R E S M A R C O R O D A R S O D
A M O U J U P R A D O L B O N U
M A R P O D I A L E M O R D E R
E S T S O N A R C A R D O R L A
R A R E P U S P O R E U S R A R
```

Ninety-five Spanish words can be made out of SUPERMERCADO. Fifty of them are in the word square. (a) See how many words you can put together with the letters in SUPERMERCADO. Letters may not be used more than once in one word unless they appear more than once in SUPERMERCADO, where there are two "e's." Although there are two "r's" you may not use a word with "rr" because that is a different letter in the Spanish alphabet. (b) Circle the words in the square and list them in the space at the bottom of the page. Continue on another sheet. Include your own additional words.

_____   _____   _____

_____   _____   _____

_____   _____   _____

9-8 SE ME HACE LA BOCA AGUA (MY MOUTH WATERS) (Vocabulary)

The names of many vegetables are listed below. Bear in mind that there are some regional variations in nomenclature for various food items. For example, in Puerto Rico "naranja" (orange) is "china"; "banana" (banana) is "guineo." In Mexico "patata" (potato) is "papa"; "pavo" (turkey) is also "guajolote." In Argentina "tocino" (bacon) is "panceta," and so it goes. . . .

LAS LEGUMBRES	VEGETABLES
el ajo (diente de ajo)	garlic (clove of garlic)
la alcachofa	artichoke
el apio	celery
la berenjena	eggplant
la calabaza	squash
el camote	sweet potato
la cebolla	onion
la col	cabbage
la coliflor	cauliflower
el champiñón (also "la seta," "el hongo")	mushroom
el elote (also "el maíz")	corn
la escarola	escarole
el espárrago	asparagus
las espinacas (always in the plural)	spinach
el garbanzo	chickpea
el guisante	pea
la habichuela verde (also "la judía")	string bean
la lechuga	lettuce
la patata	potato
el pepino	cucumber
el perejil	parsley
el pimiento	pepper
el rábano	radish
el tomate	tomato
la zanahoria	carrot

9-9 LOOK, MA, ALL VEGETABLES! (A/B)

Compose a large face using vegetables as the features (peas for the eyes, carrot for the nose, parsley for the hair, etc.). THINK VEGETABLES AND USE YOUR IMAGINATION! Bring to class a photo of your creation; name the different vegetables you used (in Spanish). The best one gets a prize!

9-10 FRUTAS (Vocabulary)

FRUTAS	FRUIT
el aguacate	avocado
el albaricoque	apricot
la banana	banana
la cereza	cherry
la ciruela	plum
el dátil	date
el durazno (also "el melocotón")	peach
la frambuesa	raspberry
la fresa	strawberry
el higo	fig
el limón	lemon
el mango	mango
la manzana	apple
el melón	melon
la naranja	orange
la pasa	raisin
la pera	pear
la piña (also "la ananá")	pineapple
el plátano (also "banana")	banana
la sandía	watermelon
la toronja	grapefruit
la uva	grape

9-11 COLORES

In the blanks supply the name of the fruit(s) of the color or description indicated.

1. A mí me gustan las frutas rojas, como _____ y _____.

2. Pepe come solamente las frutas amarillas, como _____ , _____.

3. A Manuela le gusta el color morado; así que compra muchas _____ y _____.

4. A mi hermana le gustan frutas secas, como _____ , _____ , _____.

5. Dicen que el color verde significa "esperanza"; así que me gusta comer _____ y _____.

6. Es difícil comprar una _____ porque pesa demasiado, y es difícil cargarla.

7. Los mexicanos hacen una salsa sabrosa con el _____ verde.

8. Es muy difícil mondar (pare) una _____.

9. El _____ es amarillo y la _____ también es amarilla.

9-12 FIND THE MEAT AND POULTRY

Listed below are various kinds of meat and poultry. Use the lists to help you find the words in each of the buscapalabras (puzzles) on the right.

CARNE (MEAT)

____ el biftec (steak)

____ la carne de cerdo (pork)

____ la carne de cordero (lamb)

____ la carne de res (beef)

____ la carne de ternera (veal)

____ el chorizo (sausage)

____ la hamburguesa (hamburger)

____ el hígado (liver)

____ el jamón (ham)

____ el perro caliente (hot dog)

____ el tocino (bacon)

AVES CASERAS (POULTRY)

____ la gallina (hen)

____ el pato (duck)

____ el pavo (turkey)

____ el pollo (chicken)

FIND THE MEAT

Find the meat terms in English—diagonally, vertically, horizontally, and backwards. Circle each item; the first letter is numbered. Write that number in front of its Spanish counterpart on the list.

S¹	M	B	M	A	L³	C	D	F	V⁴
O	T	S	U	V	O	B	J	E	L
P	I	E	O	W	X	Y	A	S	R
Q	N	E	A	S	B	L	M	E	L
R	O	T	L	K	T	A	G	T	Q
H⁷	C	L¹⁰	I	V	E	R	N	S	E
O	A	M	N	O	U	M	D	P	G
T	B⁶	L	M	B⁹	E	E	F	T	A
D	X	Y	M	Z	O	L	N	D	S
O	J	A	L	P	H⁵	A	M	T	U
G	H⁸	B	D	J	K	L	N	O	A
V	O	K	R	O	P²	S	V	J	S¹¹

FIND THE POULTRY

Y	E	K	R	U	T¹	N
M	T	O	Q	S	E	O
P	D³	U	C	K	L	T
A	C	B	C	H	O	N
S	O	I	T	M	J	E
L	H	Q	V	L	T	H⁴
C²	V	W	X	O	N	J

© 1996 by the Center for Applied Research in Education

9-13 SHELL ME

Circle the shellfish and check them off on the list.

<u>PESCADO</u> <u>(FISH)</u>

___ la almeja (clam)

___ la anchoa (anchovy)

___ el arenque (herring)

___ el atún (tuna)

___ el bacalao (codfish)

___ el calamar (squid)

___ el camarón (shrimp)

___ el cangrejo (crab)

___ el caracol (snail)

___ la langosta (lobster)

___ el lenguado (flounder; sole)

___ el mejillón (mussel)

___ la merluza (hake)

___ la ostra (oyster)

___ el pulpo (octopus)

___ el salmón (salmon)

___ la sardina (sardine)

___ la trucha (trout)

L	Q	P	S	T	A	R	S	O	B
N	A	T	C	I	O	N	V	P	N
C	A	N	G	R	E	J	O	L	O
A	G	O	G	C	F	H	K	M	L
R	E	R	W	O	S	T	R	A	L
A	X	A	T	R	S	J	T	R	I
C	T	M	A	O	L	T	R	I	J
O	R	A	J	E	M	L	A	N	E
L	A	C	K	B	E	F	P	A	M

9-14 OTHER FOODS (Vocabulary)

<u>VARIOS</u>	<u>VARIOUS</u>
el aceite de oliva	olive oil
la aceituna	olive
el arroz	rice
el azúcar	sugar
el batido	milkshake
el bocadillo	sandwich, snack
el cacahuate (also "el maní")	peanut
el café	coffee
el cereal	cereal
la crema	cream
los dulces	candy, sweets
el frijol (refrito)	bean (refried)
el frijol de media luna	lima bean
la galleta	cracker
la gelatina	gelatine
el guacamole	avocado dip
la harina	flour
el helado (also, "la nieve")	ice cream
el huevo (frito, pasado por agua, revuelto, duro, escalfado)	egg (fried, soft-boiled, scrambled, hard-boiled, poached)
la yema	the yolk
la clara del huevo	the white of the egg
el jugo	juice
la leche	milk
la lenteja	lentil

© 1996 by the Center for Applied Research in Education

9-14 OTHER FOODS (Vocabulary) *(continued)*

<u>VARIOS</u>	<u>VARIOUS</u>
la mantequilla	butter
la mermelada	jam, marmalade
la mayonesa	mayonnaise
los macarrones	macaroni
la miel	honey
la mostaza	mustard
la nuez	nut
el pan (tostado)	bread (toasted)
el panecillo	roll
las palomitas de maíz	popcorn
el pastel	pie, cake
el queso	cheese
el refresco	soft drink
la sal (y la pimienta)	salt (and pepper)
la salsa	sauce
la sopa	soup
el té	tea
el vinagre	vinegar

9-15 AHORA, LE TOCA A USTED

Now it is your turn to find the food items. Use the list in 9-14 to help you. There are 58 of them in the "Buscapalabras." How many can you find? Circle them and list them below with the proper definite article. Continue on another sheet if you need more space.

BUSCAPALABRAS

```
P E R E J I L     Z I A M E D A T I M O L A P C
A I         E           H A M B U R G U E S A E
L   N A R A N J A N O L E M                 T R
C   A     T       C E B O L L A             U D
A L M E J A E T O M A C         R A B A N O
C A N G R E J O         H   P
H             A C E I T U N A U   O N A T A L P
O       E T N A S I U G   V C A R A C O L
F R A M B U E S A     A A O   A S E N O Y A M
A P I O A   A J N O R O T         R E       A
T       B A T I D O   F R E S A   E S       L
G A L L I N A   Z A N A H O R I A O   S C   L I
U V A   D   O Z N A B R A G     N R   A       U
A       O M A N Z A N A         E     R       U
C A L A M A R R O L F I L O C   D     O       Q
A L B A R I C O Q U E       O S   R     L     E
M   H A B I C H U E L A T     O   N O M L A S T
O A   T E R N E R A       A   C B A C A L A O N
L H   O               C   S   N O M L A S A
E C   M A N G O     N O M I L         S     M
  U   A A T A T A P       R           L     O
  R   T       A           A A T E L L A G J
O T N E I M I P U L P O     M L A N G O S T A
```

_____ _____ _____

_____ _____ _____

_____ _____ _____

9-16 ¿Lo sabe usted?

¿Sabe usted cuál fruta fue el punto focal de las dos leyendas que siguen? Lea . . .

1. William Tell, en la leyenda suiza, era un héroe en la lucha por la independencia suiza de Austria. Para castigarlo, el gobernador austríaco le ordenó a Tell—a peligro de muerte—de lanzar una flecha a una _____ puesta en la cabeza de su hijo.

2. París, hijo de Priam, rey de Troya, otorgó la _____ a Afrodita quien, en cambio, le dio su ayuda en el rapto de Elena quien era la esposa de Menelao, rey de Esparta.

3. Y, ahora, un misterio: ¿Cuál es la fruta del árbol en el jardín del Edén, el paraíso terrestre donde vivió el primer hombre, Adán, antes de su desobediencia de no comer el fruto del árbol prohibido? Eva fue la primera en hacerlo, inducida por la mala serpiente. Luego convenció a Adán de participar porque la fruta era tan sabrosa. _____

9-17 MÁS ALIMENTOS

Circle the food items. (All of these are itemized in the vocabulary lists.) Words may go from left to right, right to left, horizontally, upward or downward, vertically, or crosswise. See how many you can find! The definite articles are not included in the word square, but please include them in your list at the bottom of the page. Some are circled for you.

BUSCAPALABRAS

G	U	A	R	E	N	R	E	T	A	I	R	A	M	E	J	I	L	L	O	N
O	A	O	H	C	N	A	X	O	L	S	A	L	P	O	Z	I	R	O	H	C
V	T	L	A	U	X	L	A	C	A	R	A	C	O	L	O	J	A	A	A	R
E	S	A	L	M	O	N	M	I	M	A	D	R	E	T	I	O	Z	U	M	O
S	A	R	P	I	S	P	E	N	A	L	O	A	L	E	G	U	A	R	B	A
E	R	M	I	N	N	A	N	O	R	E	S	C	O	L	L	A	R	A	U	B
R	D	A	R	T	I	A	R	E	N	Q	U	E	T	R	U	D	E	A	R	E
O	I	R	P	E	T	Y	A	A	K	U	S	R	E	O	V	I	D	A	G	S
A	N	O	A	R	S	O	C	S	I	R	A	M	Y	D	A	O	N	O	U	T
M	A	J	U	S	T	A	O	R	A	R	L	A	M	E	R	D	O	D	E	S
K	I	E	L	O	A	T	S	O	P	A	Y	N	H	O	B	A	R	A	S	W
A	T	R	O	P	R	A	F	C	T	H	R	A	L	C	O	G	A	U	A	D
A	M	G	S	L	T	H	O	S	R	I	A	N	T	O	I	I	M	G	R	C
J	A	N	C	U	W	R	O	I	U	D	M	A	O	L	N	H	A	N	F	E
E	L	A	N	P	D	G	Z	O	C	R	A	B	S	M	O	O	C	E	N	R
M	O	C	I	E	N	T	I	G	H	O	L	A	T	O	M	N	V	L	I	D
L	S	B	R	A	S	I	L	E	A	N	A	I	R	B	A	C	A	L	A	O
A	S	O	L	I	T	A	R	A	S	O	C	R	A	N	J	U	M	P	N	S

_____ _____ _____

_____ _____ _____

_____ _____ _____

_____ _____ _____

_____ _____ _____

_____ _____ _____

_____ _____ _____

9-18 LA PAELLA VALENCIANA—¡RICA!

La paella es una especialidad española. Viene de la costa este de España, en la región de Valencia. Aquí está uná paella valenciana. ¿Puede usted identificar en qué consiste? ¿Cuántos ingredientes puede identificar? Haga una lista con el equivalente en inglés.

_____   _____   _____

_____   _____   _____

_____   _____   _____

_____   _____   _____

_____   _____   _____

_____   _____   _____

_____   _____   _____

_____   _____   _____

_____   _____   _____

9-19 ¡PONGA LA MESA PARA EL DESAYUNO!

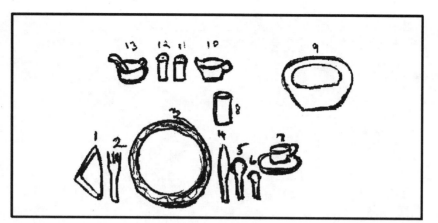

BREAKFAST, ANYONE?

Clave:

1. la servilleta
2. el tenedor
3. el plato
4. el cuchillo
5. la cuchara
6. la cucharita
7. la taza y el platillo

8. el vaso de leche
9. el plato hondo para el cereal
10. la cremera
11. el salero
12. el pimentero
13. el azucarero

De la lista de "varios," (páginas 132-133) escoja algunos alimentos que se pueden servir para el desayuno.

9-20 ¡Arrégleme!

(a) Reconstruct each sentence in proper order; (b) give the English translation; (c) list the letters circled; (d) unscramble them. They will form the name of a vegetable. What is it?

1. beber / tienen que / leche / cada día / niños / los.

   _____

   _____

2. Ⓟopeye / músculos / porque / espinacas / cada día / tiene / come.

   _____

   _____

3. el / sino / agrio / limón / dulce / Ⓔ$ / no.

   _____

   _____

4. llorar / cruda / cortar / una cebolla / muy Ⓣⓡiste / es / me hace / porque.

   _____

   _____

5. también / con / los Ⓜacarrones / y / salsa / me gusta / llamada "salsa" / me gustan / la música.

   _____

   _____

6. de Boston / la / ciudad / Ⓘnteresante / famosa / sus / es / frijoles / por.

   _____

   _____

7. no / rojo / el Ⓒolor / de / es / los pepinos.

   _____

   _____

8. crecen / no / en / las zanahoⓡias / árboles / los.

   _____

   _____

9. pescado / dice(n)que / mucho / si / vas a / muy inteligente / ser / comes.

_____

_____

10. en / fritas / sirven / patatas / Mc Donald's / ricos / otros / y / platos / hamburguesa(s)/ y.

_____

_____

Escriba aquí las letras marcadas en las frases _____

_____

¿Cuál vegetal deletrean?* _____

Haga una lista de elementos de comida mencionados en las frases precedentes. Dé el artículo definido de cada nombre.

_____   _____

_____   _____

_____   _____

_____   _____

*What vegetable do they spell?

Nombre _____ Fecha _____ **(B)**

9-21 ¿PERDER, GANAR O MANTENER?

Dé usted un desayuno apropiado.

Yo quiero perder peso. Así, para mi desayuno voy a comer: _____

_____

_____

Yo quiero ganar peso. Así, para mi desayuno voy a comer: _____

_____

_____

Yo quiero mantener el peso. Así, para mi desayuno voy a comer: _____

_____

_____

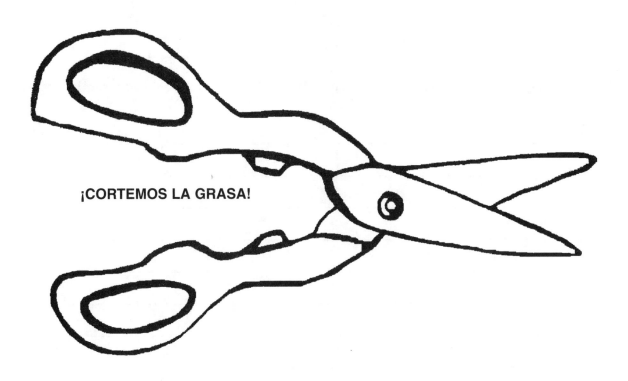

¡CORTEMOS LA GRASA!

9-22 A ALGUNOS LES GUSTA NADAR

Food items (mostly seafood) are listed horizontally backwards. List them correctly, with the definite article, giving the English equivalent.

_____   _____

_____   _____

_____   _____

_____   _____

_____   _____

_____   _____

_____   _____

_____   _____

_____   _____

Find a typical seafood dish of a Spanish region, listed vertically in the word cage; it starts with "la." Write it in the space below.

_____

9-23 No PERTENECE

En cada grupo elimine usted el elemento que no pertenece, y dé la razó n. Mire el primer ejemplo:

1. alcachofa, <u>mantequilla</u>, escarola (No es vegetal.)

2. mermelada, limón, miel

3. fresas, carne, cerezas

4. manzana, pasas, dátiles

5. aguacate, mango, cereza

6. proteína, hierro, arenque

7. camote, patata, apio

8. piña, cebolla, ajo

9. leche, crema, agua

10. sal, pan tostado, panecillo

11 cerdo, coliflor, ternera

12. toronja, naranja, albaricoque

13. arenque, merluza, pavo

14. gallina, pavo, tomate

15. almeja, langosta, trucha

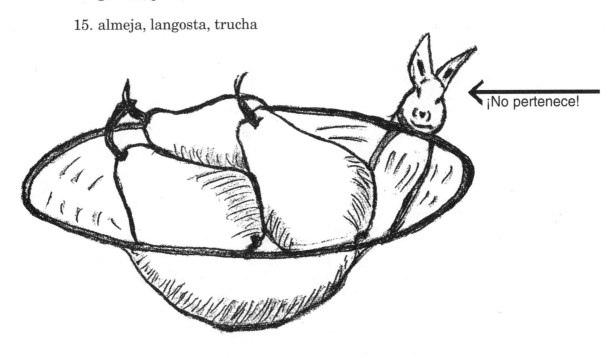

¡No pertenece!

9-24 ¡FIESTA!

The following page contains a sketch of a birthday cake surrounded by pictures of what you might do and what you might eat at a birthday party. The number of each illustration corresponds with each Spanish statement below. (a) Translate the Spanish into English. (b) By putting together the letters circled you will find out how old the young person is.

1. Damos regalos.   _____

2. Cantamos canciones.   _____

3. Bailamos.   _____

4. Tocamos el piano.   _____

5. Comemos galletas con salsa picante.   _____

6. Comemos dulces.   _____

7. Comemos hojuelas de patatas fritas.   _____

8. Comemos frutas: peras, bananas, manzanas, uvas. _____

9. Comemos perros calientes.   _____

10. Comemos palomitas de maíz.   _____

11. Comemos helado.   _____

    Las letras con círculos son: _____

    La persona festejada tiene   _____ años.

© 1996 by the Center for Applied Research in Education

Tarta de cumpleaños,
con velas

¡FELIZ CUMPLEAÑOS!

9-25 ¿QUÉ SE COMPRA?

¿Qué se compra en estas tiendas? Escriba en frases completas: "En la carnicería se compra carne."

la carnicería _____

la cafetería _____

la frutería _____

la heladería _____

la lechería _____

la panadería _____

la pastelería _____

el supermercado _____

Otros:

la bodega: En países latino-americanos se compran varios alimentos en la bodega. En España la bodega es un lugar donde se guarda el vino.

la pulquería: En la pulquería se compra pulque, una bebida espiritosa hecha del jugo fermentado de la planta agave. El pulque se usa en México.

9-26 ¿QUÉ VAS A PREPARAR?

Su mejor amigo quiere preparar una comida típicamente norteamericana para un grupo de amigos hispanos. ¿Qué sugerencias (suggestions) puede usted hacerle?

aperitivo (appetizer) _____

_____

plato principal (main dish) _____

_____

otros (others: vegetables, salad, bread and butter, soda, etc.) _____

_____

postre (dessert) _____

_____

¿A qué hora vienen los invitados? _____

_____

Section 10

HOGAR Y FAMILIA
(HOME AND FAMILY)

Be it ever so humble there is no place like home.
(Por humilde que sea, no hay ningún lugar como el hogar.)

John Howard Payne (1791–1852)

- Conozca usted a la familia hispana.

- Una merienda campestre

- Ir de camping

- Cuartos, muebles y componentes de una casa

- Los quehaceres domésticos

- Los niños van a la escuela.

10-1 CONOZCA USTED A LA FAMILIA HISPANA
(Vocabulario, nota cultural y traducción)

los parientes	relatives	el tío abuelo	great uncle
el marido, el esposo	husband	la tía abuela	great aunt
la mujer, la esposa	wife	el nieto	grandson
el matrimonio	married couple	la nieta	granddaughter
el padre (papá)	father (papa)	los nietos	grandchildren (m. & f.)
la madre (mamá)	mother (mama)	el bisnieto	great-grandson
los padres	parents	la bisnieta	great-granddaughter
el abuelo	grandfather	los bisnietos	great-grandchildren (m. & f.)
la abuela	grandmother	el sobrino	nephew
los abuelos	grandparents	la sobrina	niece
el bisabuelo	great-grandfather	los sobrinos	nieces and nephews
la bisabuela	great-grandmother	la resobrina	great niece
los bisabuelos	great-grandparents	el resobrino	great nephew
el hijo	son	el suegro	father-in-law
la hija	daughter	la suegra	mother-in-law
los hijos	children (m.& f.)	el padrastro	stepfather
el hermano	brother	la madrastra	stepmother
la hermana	sister	el hermanastro	stepbrother
los hermanos	brothers and sisters	la hermanastra	stepsister
el primo, la prima	cousin	el cuñado	brother-in-law
el tío	uncle	la cuñada	sister-in-law
la tía	aunt		

10-1 CONOZCA USTED A LA FAMILIA HISPANA (Vocabulario, nota cultural y traducción) *(continued)*

Nota cultural: Translate these paragraphs into English in the space provided.

En la sociedad hispana el honor familiar es muy importante. Los jóvenes hispanos son el orgullo (pride) de sus padres, de sus abuelos y de sus parientes. Es su deber mantener el honor familiar.

Las reuniones familiares son muy frecuentes. Hay una gran comida para celebrar los días de fiesta. Hijos y padres van juntos al campo, a la playa, al teatro y al museo. Así la familia se mantiene muy unida. También, un buen amigo de los hijos es amigo de toda la familia.

_____

_____

_____

_____

_____

_____

_____

_____

_____

_____

10-2 ¿QUIÉN ES?

Dé usted el parentesco (relationship) según la explicación:

1. Jorge es hijo de mis padres. Es mi _____.

2. Elena es hija de mi tía. Es mi _____.

3. Mario y Juan son hijos de mi tío. Son mis _____.

4. Enrique es hijo de mi hermano. Es mi _____.

5. Tomás García es el padre de mi madre. Es mi _____.

6. Juan Ponce es el padre de mi abuela. Es mi _____.

7. Lola es la esposa de mi padre, pero no es mi madre. Es mi _____.

8. Gloria es hija de mi madrastra. Es mi _____.

9. El marido de mi hermana es mi _____.

10. Los padres de mi marido son mis _____.

11. La hija de mi hermano es mi _____.

12. Los hijos de mi nieta son mis _____.

13. La hija de mi sobrina es mi _____.

14. Juan e Isabelita son hijos de mi hijo. Son mis _____.

10-3 UNA MERIENDA CAMPESTRE

VOCABULARIO

- ✓ ir de merienda (to go on a picnic)

  están desayunándose (They are having breakfast.)

- ✓ ¡Chévere! (Super! Great!)

  ¡Hagámoslo! (Let's do it. [command])

- ✓ la canasta de comestibles (the basket of food)

- ✓ revisar (to check over)

  búsquelos (Look for them! [command])

  además de (in addition to)

- ✓ la despensa (pantry)

- ✓ la lechuga (lettuce)

- ✓ las zanahorias (carrots)

- ✓ las manzanas (apples)

  las uvas (grapes)

- ✓ la tortilla (omelet)

- ✓ las palomitas de maíz (popcorn)

- ✓ las patatas fritas (potato chips)

  el postre (dessert)

- ✓ las hormigas (ants)

  molestar (to bother, annoy)

  A ver (Let's see.)

© 1996 by the Center for Applied Research in Education

10-3 UNA MERIENDA CAMPESTRE *(continued)*

DIÁLOGO

Hoy es día de fiesta. La familia González—padre, madre e hijos, Carlos y María—están desayunándose.

Sr. G.: Hace buen tiempo hoy. ¿Por qué no vamos de merienda al campo?

Carlos: ¡Chévere, papá! ¡Hagámoslo!

Sra. G.: De acuerdo. María, ¿quieres ayudarme a preparar una canasta de comestibles? A ver qué tenemos en el refrigerador.

María: Sí, mamá. (Abre la puerta del refrigerador.) Pues, hay un buen pedazo de jamón; hay huevos, lechuga, tomates, zanahorias, manzanas, uvas y ¿qué te parece? ¡Hay una cajita de chocolates!

Sra. G.: ¡Bien! ¡Bien! Vamos a preparar una tortilla de huevos y jamón y vegetales, una ensalada de lechuga y tomates, y de postre, chocolates y frutas. ¿Qué más?

Carlos: Ay, mamá, ¿podemos comprar palomitas de maíz y patatas fritas?

Sra. G.: Sí, está bien. Vete con papá al supermercado, y compren pan también.

Sr. G.: Primero, tenemos que revisar el coche, Carlos. Creo que necesita gasolina.

Sra. G.: Un momentito. Vamos a ver si tenemos vasos y servilletas de papel. María, búscalos en la despensa, por favor.

María: No hay ni lo uno ni lo otro, mamá.

Sra. G.: Entonces, sí, necesitamos vasos y servilletas de papel además de palomitas de maíz, hojuelos de patatas fritas y pan.

Sr. G.: Vamos de compras, Carlos.
(A su mujer y a María les dice): Ah, y no se olviden de preparar algo para las hormigas; así no nos van a molestar.

Cultural Note: It is a Spanish custom to have two surnames. The first is the father's; the second is the mother's. When a woman marries she drops the second surname (mother's); so if María Montero Ayala marries Miguel Ortiz Pérez, she will be named María Montero de Ortiz. The children will be named Pablo and Matilde Ortiz Montero. Today some women prefer not to use the "de" in front of the husband's name.

© 1996 by the Center for Applied Research in Education

10-4 La familia González

Refiriéndose al diálogo en 10-3, escriba usted las respuestas a las preguntas, en frases completas.

1. ¿Cuántas personas hay en la familia González?

_____

2. Al comienzo del diálogo ¿qué están haciendo?

_____

3. ¿Hace mal tiempo en ese día de fiesta?

_____

4. ¿Qué propone (suggest) el Sr. González?

_____

5. ¿Están de acuerdo todos?

_____

6. ¿Quiénes van a preparar la merienda?

_____

7. Mientras tanto ¿qué van a hacer el Sr. González y Carlos?

_____

8. ¿Qué tienen que comprar el Sr. González y Carlos en el supermercado?

_____

9. Antes de irse ¿qué les dice el Sr. González a su mujer y a María?

_____

10. ¿Cree usted que las hormigas tienen derecho de comer también? Explique.

_____

HOGAR Y FAMILIA

© 1996 by the Center for Applied Research in Education

10-5 Ir de camping

Traduzca:

Es un fin de semana largo, y la familia González—madre, padre e hijos, Carlos y María—van a ir de camping. En las preparaciónes, están juntando los requisitos indispensables. Además de la ropa y la comida que la señora González y María están preparando, en esta excursión se necesita:

una tienda de campaña   una sartén

un saco de dormir   una linterna eléctrica

una mochila   unos gemelos de campo

una manta

Después de mucha conmoción (excitement), todo está listo, y mañana al alba (dawn) se pondrán en camino. (They will start out.)

10-6 ¡Olé!

In the following block of letters find twelve words (or groups of words) taken from the "vocabulario" which precedes the dialogue "una merienda campestre." (The words used in the square are checked.) Circle the words as you find them. They may be written forward, backward, diagonally, or upside down. You will be given a certain amount of time to complete the search. The first student to find all the words shouts "olé" and wins the contest.

C	O	O	A	D	N	E	I	R	E	M	E	D	R	I	L
A	H	S	L	M	O	P	Q	E	D	O	L	M	A	I	M
N	L	E	S	T	R	T	B	V	C	A	R	B	A	S	N
A	O	T	V	S	M	O	L	I	B	I	P	O	U	O	U
S	M	A	T	E	I	M	N	S	A	L	A	N	E	A	V
T	X	W	Z	T	R	O	S	A	O	O	T	T	I	V	W
A	B	D	F	G	I	E	K	R	M	E	A	R	R	T	Y
D	E	S	P	E	N	S	A	L	L	I	T	R	O	T	X
E	A	C	O	M	N	R	T	V	X	C	A	T	S	O	T
C	L	O	V	U	I	O	Q	T	R	B	S	U	H	P	L
O	L	P	W	M	O	W	U	B	C	A	F	O	I	O	S
M	A	N	Z	A	N	A	S	O	S	T	R	B	C	R	A
E	R	A	M	V	G	O	M	N	I	M	I	N	M	U	I
S	Q	U	V	U	C	V	W	P	I	U	T	L	L	A	R
T	O	M	H	P	O	S	T	G	W	X	A	S	E	B	O
I	R	C	I	T	S	W	A	A	M	N	S	O	C	C	H
B	E	I	A	U	P	S	V	Q	R	L	N	M	M	F	A
L	V	M	B	C	T	D	E	G	H	O	F	A	O	G	N
E	R	P	U	S	D	E	G	N	O	P	Q	S	G	O	A
S	P	A	L	O	M	I	T	A	S	D	E	M	A	I	Z

10-7 ¿PARA QUÉ SIRVE?

Complete the sentences below.

1. La familia González se está preparando para _____.

2. Una mochila se usa para _____.

3. Una manta se usa para _____.

4. Una sartén se usa para _____.

5. Una linterna eléctrica se usa para _____.

6. Los gemelos de campo se usan para _____.

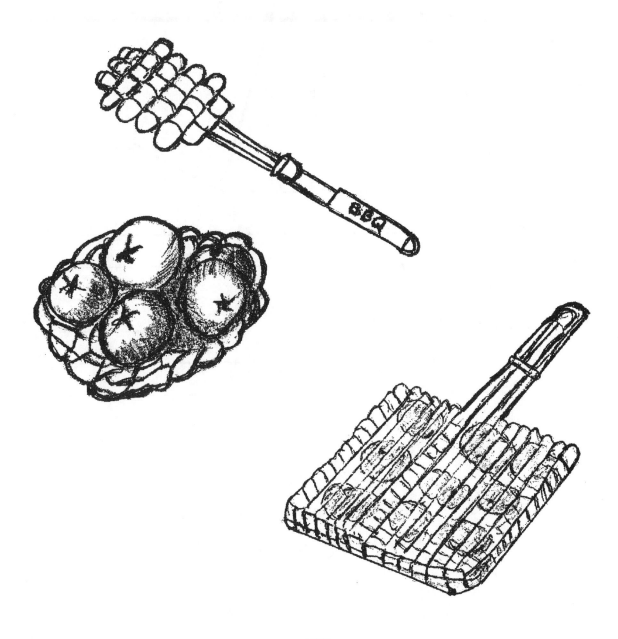

10-8 MÁS UTENSILIOS

Además de los artículos ya mencionados, hay otros que son útiles cuando se va de camping. Hagan ustedes una lista y discutan en clase porqué se necesitan esos artículos.

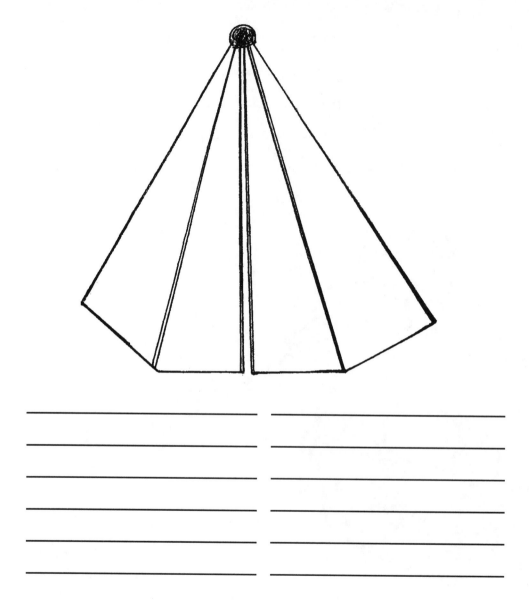

_____   _____

_____   _____

_____   _____

_____   _____

_____   _____

_____   _____

10-9 CUARTOS, MUEBLES Y COMPONENTES DE UNA CASA

Traduzca:

En general, un cuarto consiste en cuatro paredes, un techo, un suelo, unas ventanas y una puerta.

En la puerta de entrada hay la cadena de seguridad, la mirilla (peephole) y el buzón de cartas.

En el dormitorio hay una cama con un colchón, almohadas, una frazada, una cubrecama, una silla, un sillón, una mesita de noche y una lámpara. En la ventana hay cortinas. En la mesita de noche hay un despertador; además hay una cómoda, un tocador y un ropero con un espejo.

En la sala de estar hay un sofá, unas butacas, un escritorio, unos estantes para libros o baratijas, un televisor, un equipo de sonido, lámparas y cuadros.

En el comedor hay una mesa con mantel, unas sillas y un aparador.

En la cocina hay unos armarios, una aspiradora, una escoba, un refrigerador, una lavadora de ropa, una lavadora de platos, una secadora, un congelador, una estufa y un ventilador. Otros aparatos eléctricos: una licuadora, una tostadora, un abrelatas, una radio.

En el cuarto de baño hay una bañera, una ducha, unos aparatos sanitarios (bathroom fittings), toallas de baño, paños para lavarse, una alfombra de baño y azulejos. Otros artículos: las zapatillas de baño, el jabón de baño, los polvos de baño, la bata de baño (bathrobe), el gorro de baño.

En una casa particular hay una escalera que lleva al sótano, un garaje para el coche y los utensilios de jardinería y un jardín.

10-10 Díme . . .

Fill in the blanks.

1. Generalmente un cuarto tiene (four walls) _____ .

2. Cervantes en "Don Quijote" dice que (the walls have ears)

   _____ .

3. La (peephole) _____ en la (entrance door)

   _____ sirve para ver quién llama a la puerta.

4. En la (bed) _____ hay un (mattress) _____ ,

   unas (pillows) _____ , una (blanket) _____ y

   una (bedspread) _____ .

5. El (alarm clock) _____ se pone en la (night table)

   _____ .

6. Me gusta sentarme en una (armchair) _____ en la (family

   room) _____ .

7. La cena se sirve en el (dining room) _____ .

8. El (refrigerator) _____ está en la (kitchen)

   _____ .

9. Para mantener la ropa limpia necesitamos una (washing machine)

   _____ .

10. En la cocina hay varios (electrical appliances) _____ .

11. La (bathtub) _____ y la (shower) _____ están

    en el (bathroom) _____ .

12. En una (private home) _____ hay un (basement)

    _____ y un (garage) _____ .

10-11 LOS QUEHACERES DOMÉSTICOS

Un buen miembro de familia es responsable. Ayuda en los quehaceres de la casa. Escucha cuando le hablan. No critica a otros. Considera los sentimientos de otros. Ayuda en resolver los problemas de la familia. Cuida a los hermanos pequeños. Limpia y arregla su cuarto. Saca a caminar al perro. Cuando posible, ayuda al ama de casa en:

ir de compras	to shop
cocinar	to cook
poner la mesa	to set the table
lavar los platos	to wash the dishes
limpiar la cocina	to clean the kitchen
fregar el piso	to scrub the floor
limpiar el cuarto de baño	to clean the bathroom
quitar el polvo a los muebles	to dust the furniture
limpiar las alfombras	to vacuum the rugs
planchar la ropa	to iron the clothes
sacar la basura	to take out the garbage

VOCABULARIO

el comedor	(dining room)
las servilletas	(napkins)
los tenedores	(forks)
las cucharas	(spoons)
los panecillos	(rolls)
¡Válgame Dios!	(For goodness' sake!)
retelleno	(lleno = full; rete-= extremely; very, very full)
Le toca a Silvia.	(It's Silvia's turn.)
está quejándose	(is complaining)

© 1996 by the Center for Applied Research in Education

10-11 LOS QUEHACERES DOMÉSTICOS *(continued)*

DIÁLOGO: COOPERACIÓN FAMILIAR

Es domingo y la familia Fernández—padre, madre, Silvia y Manolo—van a cenar. La señora Fernández está en la cocina preparando la comida. Silvia está en el comedor poniendo la mesa. Manolo está jugando con Bobo, el perro, y el señor Fernández está leyendo el periódico.

Silvia:	¡Ya está! (There!) Los platos, las servilletas, los tenedores, las cucharas, los cuchillos, los vasos para el agua, la mantequilla, los panecillos.
Señora F.:	¡Válgame Dios! El bote de basura está retelleno. Manolo, por favor, llévalo afuera.
Manolo:	¡Uf! ¿Por qué siempre yo tengo que hacer esa tarea?
Silvia:	Siempre está quejándose.
	(Después de la comida el señor F. le dice a Manolo:) Es hora de sacar a Bobo a caminar.
Manolo:	Papá, le toca a Silvia esta vez.
Señor F.:	Tu hermana está ayudando a tu madre. Sé más responsable!

¿CIERTO O FALSO? (COOPERACIÓN FAMILIAR)

Refiriéndose al diálogo, si la frase es verdad, escriba usted "cierto"; si no lo es, escriba "falso" y escriba la frase correcta.

1. La señora Fernández está bailando. _____

   _____

2. Silvia está rompiendo los platos. _____

   _____

3. El Señor Fernández está mirando la televisión. _____

   _____

4. Manolo está jugando con el perro. _____

   _____

5. Manolo nunca se queja. _____

   _____

NO DEBO. . .

In order to make a more perfect family there are two things that the children—Manolo and Silvia—should not do. Unscramble the verbs:

Manolo no debe   jarquees   _____

Silvia no debe   raccriti   _____

10-12 ¿DÓNDE ESTÁ MI LUGAR?

On the next page you will find a word square containing 15 household items. The words are horizontally, vertically, or diagonally placed. Circle each one; then write them in the spaces below where they will correctly complete each sentence.

1. Pongo mi ropa en el _ _ _ _ _ _ .

2. María prepara la cena en la _ _ _ _ _ _ .

3. Para cenar, nos sentamos en la mesa en el _ _ _ _ _ _ _ _ .

4. Los niños se lavan las manos en el _ _ _ _ _ _ _ _ _ _ _ _ _ _ .

5. Después de la comida tomamos café en la _ _ _ _ _ _ _ _ _ _ _ _ .

6. A los invitados les gusta ver las flores en el _ _ _ _ _ _ _ .

7. Mi padre tiene botellas de vino en el _ _ _ _ _ _ _ .

8. Mi coche está en el _ _ _ _ _ _ _ .

9. Nuestros invitados se acuestan en el _ _ _ _ _ _ _ _ _ _ _ .

10. Mi madre limpia las alfombras con una _ _ _ _ _ _ _ _ _ _ _ _ .

11. En la sala de estar me siento en el _ _ _ _ _ .

12. Las cortinas cubren las _ _ _ _ _ _ _ _ _ .

13. Mi padre se afeita (shaves) mirándose en el _ _ _ _ _ _ _ .

14. Los cuadros se ponen en las _ _ _ _ _ _ _ _ .

15. El niño se sienta en una pequeña _ _ _ _ _ _ .

Note: The number of dashes indicates the number of letters in each word.

10-13 ¡BÚSQUEME!

There are 15 household words in the square. Find them, circle them, and list them; include the definite articles.

```
A R O D A R I P S A V
M O C O M E D O R J E
R M U O T U F V W O N
A N A A C A S O T S T
T W R L P I J A E U A
S Z T L C E N D F B N
E G O I P L E A T L A
E A D S O R C P U M S
D R E V A A O O V W O
A A B P L M S P O R T
L J A R D I N Q E T A
A E Ñ L N B W X Y R N
S D O R M I T O R I O
```

_____

_____

_____

_____

_____

_____

_____

_____

_____

_____

_____

_____

_____

_____

10-14 School and Study (Vocabulary)

Actividades de todos los días:

> estudiar (matemáticas, español, inglés, etc.) cuidadosamente
>
> contestar en clase (answer in class)
>
> aprender algo interesante (learn something interesting)
>
> hacer la tarea todos los días (do your homework every day)
>
> sacar buenas notas (get good grades)
>
> no perder el tiempo (not to waste time)
>
> no dormirse en clase (not to sleep in class)
>
> tener buenos modales (be polite)
>
> obedecer y respetar a los maestros(as) (obey and respect the teachers)

Vocabulario

> estar de vacaciones (to be on vacation)
>
> ¡Requetebién! (Great!)
>
> el bosque (the woods)
>
> la piscina (the pool)
>
> ¡Dichoso tú! (Lucky you!)
>
> ¿De veras? (Really?)
>
> ¡Aquí estamos! (Here we are!)
>
> al salir (at dismissal time)
>
> ¡Hasta luego! (So long! See you later!)

10-15 Traduzca: El primer día del semestre

Manuel y su amigo Alberto están en camino a la escuela.

Manuel: ¿Estás contento de volver a la escuela?

Alberto: Pues, sí y no. Prefiero estar de vacaciones.

Manuel: Sí, yo también. ¿Cómo has pasado las vacaciones?

Alberto: ¡Requetebién! Pasé unas semanas con mi primo quien vive en el campo. Nos divertimos mucho caminando por el bosque, nadando en la piscina y jugando al tenis. Además, mi tía es una buena cocinera.

Manuel: Pues, dichoso tú. Nosotros nos quedamos en la ciudad. Creo que hoy vamos a recibir nuestros programas de estudio para el nuevo semestre.

Alberto: Puede ser. ¿Sacaste buenas notas el semestre pasado?

Manuel: Más o menos, pero en la química no salí muy bien.

Alberto: En mi caso, la historia me dió problemas. Voy a dejar el juego de fútbol para concentrarme más en mis estudios.

Manuel: ¿De veras? Pues, ¡aquí estamos! Te veo más tarde. Espérame al salir.

Alberto: Está bien. ¡Hasta luego!

10-16 SCHOOL AND STUDY

VOCABULARIO ÚTIL

> aprender de memoria (memorize)
>
> la campanilla (school bell)
>
> el campo de recreo (playground)
>
> el cuaderno (notebook)
>
> los cursos (courses)
>
> el director (principal)
>
> encontrar dificultad con la lengua (have difficulty with the language)
>
> el gimnasio (gymnasium)
>
> la goma (pencil eraser)
>
> el papel (paper)
>
> el reloj (clock)
>
> salir bien en ciencia (do well in science)
>
> la tiza (chalk)

Traduzca:

En los países hispanos la disciplina escolar es más fuerte que en los Estados Unidos. El alumno es castigado si llega tarde a la escuela y si no hace la tarea. Hay varios castigos, incluso pasar el sábado en la escuela.

10-17 ROMPECABEZAS: PALABRAS ESCOLÁSTICAS

There are 15 horizontal words in the word square; they are given in English at the bottom of the square. Give the Spanish equivalent. If you write the correct word in the right place (next to each number on the square), the circled, vertical area in the square will spell an adverb, an adjective, and a noun equalling something that all students want. What is it?

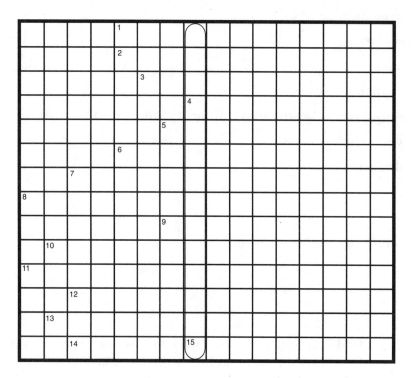

1. chemistry
2. studies (n.)
3. today
4. fountain pen
5. student's desk in a classroom
6. paper
7. school bell
8. program

9. school
10. notebook
11. gymnasium
12. principal of the school
13. computer
14. course
15. semester

What do all students want? _____

VIAJAR (TRAVEL)

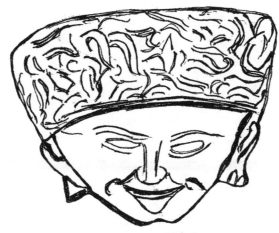

escultura maya, México

llama de los Andes

V
I
A
J
A
R

pato bobo, las Galápagos, Ecuador

baile flamenco, España

vendedor ambulante, Perú

mate y bombilla, Argentina

11-1 ¡Buen viaje! (Background)

Your passport is your "open sesame" to foreign countries. In most Spanish-speaking countries you will not need a visa, which is a stamp on your passport granting entry into that country. If you take a class trip, your teacher will be your guide and interpreter and will answer your questions. In addition, your guidebook and a dictionary will supply you with a lot of information.

In your travels you may see in some places interesting sights—donkeys doing the work of delivery trucks, men and women carrying all kinds of heavy bundles on their heads and shoulders. In the same place, you may also see modern automobiles, trucks, and taxis as in many cities in the world.

The Hispanic world is basically similar to any other, aside from its different geographic, climatic, and political aspects. There is a growing middle class, and in many areas technology is also progressing fairly rapidly.

You will notice an overall, interesting characteristic. For example, if you shop for ceramics, you will not find two objects exactly alike. Artisans take pride in producing individual artifacts.

Travelling through any of the Spanish-speaking countries you will enjoy its magnificent natural beauty—the Cantabrian Mountains of northern Spain, the high Andes of Chile, the snowy volcanoes of Mexico, the grassy plains of Argentina, South America's famous Iguazú Falls, the Roman ruins in Spain, also its Moorish palaces and Gothic cathedrals. In Spanish America, from Mexico to Peru, you will see impressive ruins of Incan, Aztec, and Mayan civilizations overthrown by the Spaniards. Enjoy it all—and SPEAK SPANISH! ¡Buen viaje!

11-2 Vocabulario turístico

el avión (airplane)   el boleto aéreo (airplane ticket)

el vuelo (the flight)   el equipaje (luggage)

la partida (departure)   la maleta (suitcase)

el piloto (pilot)   la aduana (customs)

el/la auxiliar de vuelo (flight attendant)   el pasaporte (passport)

la azafata (stewardess)   pasar por la aduana (go through customs)

el aeropuerto (airport)   objetos perdidos (Lost and Found)

el despegue (the takeoff)   el autobús, ómnibus (bus)

el aterrizaje (the landing)   el coche cama (Pullman sleeper)

la carreta (luggage cart)   libre de aduana (duty-free)

Complete the following sentences using the above vocabulary.

¡COMPLÉTEME!

1. _____ del avión se retrasó (delayed) por la niebla (fog).

2. Para viajar en avión se necesita un _____ .

3. Encontré mi cartera (pocketbook) en los _____ .

4. En el _____ compramos artículos _____ .

5. Cargamos nuestro _____ en una _____ .

6. _____ les da información a los pasajeros.

7. El _____ nos ayuda con los paquetes.

8. Dormí bien en el _____ del tren.

9. Después del aterrizaje es necesario _____ .

11-3 UN VIAJE DE NOVIOS

Lolita y Paco van a pasar la segunda luna de miel en México. Van a empezar su viaje mañana por la mañana. Están preparando sus maletas.

Lolita:	Amor, ¿quieres que te ayude con tu maleta?
Paco:	No, gracias, ya está.
Lolita:	¡Ay, estoy tan entusiasmada! Vamos a ver tantas cosas interesantes en Guadalajara, Veracruz y Tampico.
Paco:	Sí, y Mérida en la península de Yucatán, Chichen Itzá, donde hay ruinas de la cultura maya, y Taxco, ciudad antigua donde voy a comprarte un regalito de plata.
Lolita:	¡No me digas! Y no olvidemos Acapulco donde hay esas famosas playas de la costa del Pacífico.
Paco:	¡Ah, qué recreo nadar, nadar, nadar!
Lolita:	Sí, claro. Y no te olvides las cosas interesantes que hay en la Ciudad de México—el Palacio de Bellas Artes, donde vamos a ver esos famosos murales de Diego Rivera y otros artistas sobresalientes; la Basílica de Guadalupe, fundada en honor de la Virgen de Guadalupe, santa patrona del país; y muy cerca están los jardines flotantes de Xochimilco.
Paco:	(Olfateando) Amor, ¡huelo algo!
Lolita:	¡Dios mío, se está quemando la comida!

VOCABULARIO

la segunda luna de miel (second honeymoon)

mañana por la mañana (tomorrow morning)

ya está (It's all ready.)

entusiasmada (very excited)

la cultura maya (Mayan culture)

¡No me digas! (You don't say! Really?)

regalito de plata (a little silver gift)

artistas sobresalientes (outstanding artists)

santa patrona (patron saint)

los jardines flotantes (floating gardens)

olfateando (sniffing the air)

huelo algo (I smell something.)

se está quemando (is burning)

11-3 UN VIAJE DE NOVIOS (continued)

¡IDENTIFÍQUEME!

In the dialogue Lolita and Paco mention a number of places they are going to visit in México. They are listed below BUT they have to be unscrambled.

oicampt _____   mcoéxi _____

nátucay _____   chenich záit _____

zucrvare _____   ctaxo _____

copulaca _____   idaerm _____

uadalgjara _____

11-4 Stopping Places in Spanish-Speaking Countries

As you travel you will find different types of accommodations. A <u>posada</u>, a <u>parador</u>, and an <u>albergue</u> are similar to a motel or an inn. An <u>hostería</u> only serves meals, no lodging, and it is generally situated along a highway. A <u>refugio</u> is a hotel situated in a mountain area.

Those who serve in a hotel:

<u>el</u> <u>mozo</u> (porter): Takes your luggage to the registration office when you enter or leave. After you return the keys to your room,

<u>el</u> <u>dependiente</u> (clerk) will give you the bill for your room and services. The porter will call a taxi in which he will deposit your luggage.

<u>el</u> <u>botones</u> (bellhop): Follows orders and does errands.

<u>el</u> <u>camarero</u> (waiter): Serves coffee and meals in the restaurant.

<u>propinas</u> (tipping): Varies from country to country. Inquire as to what is customary.

Note: Services may vary from place to place.

Complete usted las frases siguientes.

1. En un restaurante el _____ sirve la comida. Si usted está satisfecho

   con el servicio, le deja una _____ .

2. En un hotel el _____ sigue órdenes y lleva recados (delivers

   messages). Se llama así porque tiene muchos _____ en la chaqueta.

3. El _____ le ayuda con el equipaje.

4. En un hotel el _____ le da la llave de su cuarto.

5. En una _____ generalmente sirven solamente comidas.

11-5 Diálogo: En el hotel

VOCABULARIO

¿En qué puedo servirle? (May I help you?)

el piso (floor)

con vista a la calle (with a view of the street)

tranquilo (quiet)

tocar el timbre (to ring the bell, buzzer)

un rato (a while)

el ascensor (elevator)

Me quedo con éste. (I'll take this one.)

bajemos (Let's go down. [command])

haga el favor (Please do me the favor. [command])

Traduzca:

Recepcionista:	Buenos días. ¿En qué puedo servirle?
Sr. López:	Quisiera un cuarto para una persona.
Recep.:	¿En qué piso lo quiere usted, y por cuánto tiempo?
Sr. López:	Por tres días. Prefiero el último piso, y con vista a la calle. ¿Puede usted enseñarme uno?
Recep.:	¡Por supuesto! Con mucho gusto. Subimos en el ascensor.
Sr. López:	¿Están bien ventilados los cuartos?
Recep.:	Sí, sí, y tranquilos también. (El recepcionista le muestra el cuarto. El señor López lo examina.)
Sr. López:	Está bien. Parece cómodo. Me quedo con éste.
Recep.:	Bien. Entonces bajemos y le doy la llave; usted me hará el favor de firmar el libro de registro. Si necesita algo, haga el favor de tocar el timbre.
Sr. López:	Muchas gracias. Por el momento no quiero nada más. Voy a descansar un rato.

11-6 Crucigrama

Under the square is a list of English words. Write their Spanish equivalents in the corresponding number square. List the letters that are in the circled boxes. Unscramble them. They will give you the name of a hotel employee. Write that name in the longest line of vertical boxes in the square.

HORIZONTAL

1. elevator

2. view (n.)

3. register (n.)

4. room

5. to rest (v.)

6. street

VERTICAL

7. person

8. floor

9. bell, buzzer

Circled letters: _____

Hotel employee: _____

11-7 Quisiera ir . . . .

List the Spanish-speaking countries you would like to visit in the left-hand column and why you would like to visit those countries in the right-hand column.

PAÍS   INTERÉS

AUTOMÓVILES (AUTOMOBILES)

**¡Póngase el cinturón
de seguridad!**

¡Pare!

¡Siga derecho!

¡Ceda el paso!

¡Atención al semáforo!

¡Se prohibe el paso!

12-1 ALQUILAR UN AUTO

Juan y su amigo, Luis, están en San José, capital de Costa Rica, y quieren hacer una excursión por los alrededores de la ciudad. Van a una agencia de automóviles.

Agente: ¿En qué puedo servirle?
Juan: Queremos alquilar, por una semana, un coche automático, con aire acondicionado.
Agente: Su licencia de conducir, por favor.
Juan: Aquí la tiene.
Agente: Haga el favor de esperar unos minutos. (En diez minutos regresa con un auto de color verde.) ¿Les gusta éste? Ya está revisado y tiene gasolina en el tanque, agua en el radiador, y las llantas tienen bastante aire.
Juan: ¿Te gusta, Luis?
Luis: Sí, me parece muy bien.
Juan: ¿Cuánto debemos pagar?
Agente: Pues, un depósito de garantía, y al entregar el coche usted paga el importe total.

VOCABULARIO

alquilar (to rent)

los alrededores (the environs)

está revisado (It is checked out.)

un depósito de garantía (a security deposit)

al entregar (upon returning [the car])

el importe total (total charge)

Dé usted las respuestas a las preguntas siguientes:

1. ¿Dónde están Juan y Luis? _____

   _____

2. ¿Para qué quieren alquilar un coche? _____

   _____

3. ¿De qué color es el coche que escogieron? _____

   _____

4. ¿Le falta aire en las llantas? _____

   _____

5. ¿Está vacío el tanque de gasolina? _____

   _____

6. ¿Necesita agua el radiador? _____

   _____

7. ¿Para qué necesitan un coche con aire acondicionado? _____

   _____

12-2 PARTES DEL AUTO

la capota (top)	la llanta (tire)
la ventanilla (window)	la rueda de delante (front wheel)
el picaporte (handle)	el parachoques (bumper)
la cerradura (lock)	la placa (license plate)
el baúl (trunk)	la luz delantera (headlight)
el parabrisas (windshield)	la luz trasera (rear light)
la rueda de atrás (back wheel)	el volante (steering wheel)
la cubierta del motor (hood)	el espejo (mirror)

Look at this sketch of a car. On the vertical and horizontal lines provided write, in Spanish, the names of the different parts indicated. Use the preceding vocabulary list.

(el automóvil, auto, coche, carro)

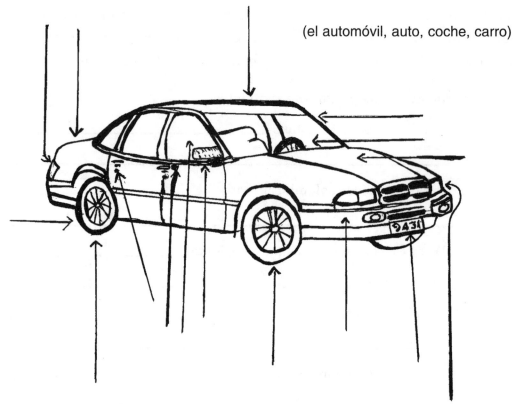

With apologies to William Shakespeare:
A car by any other name is still a car.

12-3 GOOD-DRIVING RULES

Below are 11 good-driving rules (in Spanish). English translations follow this list.
Pair the number of the English meaning with the Spanish statement.

Example:

1. **Conozca bien el código de tránsito.** _____2_____

2. Párese ante los peatones. _____

3. Quédese tranquilo(a) en toda ocasión. _____

4. Conduzca despacio en el pueblo. _____

5. Conduzca más de prisa en la carretera. _____

6. Obedezca el semáforo. _____

7. Ponga atención a las señales de tránsito. _____

8. Al ver la luz roja, párese. _____

9. Ponga las luces direccionales antes de doblar la esquina. _____

10. Si hay necesidad de llamar atención, toque la bocina. _____

11. Mantenga limpio el parabrisas. _____

BUENOS CONSEJOS DE CONDUCIR

(1) Keep the windshield clean.

(2) Know the traffic rules.

(3) If it is necessary to attract attention, blow the horn.

(4) Stop before pedestrians.

(5) Pay attention to road signs.

(6) Obey the traffic lights.

(7) Stay calm under all circumstances.

(8) Upon seeing a red light, stop.

(9) Turn on the directional signal before you turn corners.

(10) Drive slowly in towns.

(11) Drive at greater speed on the highways.

12-4 HERRAMIENTAS ÚTILES

¿Qué hace el mecánico en la estación de servicio?

Llena el tanque con gasolina. (Fills the gas tank.)

Cambia el aceite. (Changes the oil.)

Arregla los frenos. (Adjusts the brakes.)

Pone agua en el radiador. (Adds water to the radiator.)

Limpia el parabrisas. (Cleans the windshield.)

Pone aire en las llantas. (Puts air in the tires.)

Revisa la rueda de recambio. (Checks the spare tire.)

El mecánico le dice al dueño del auto que sería buena idea tener estas herramientas
en el baúl, por si acaso (just in case.)

HERRAMIENTAS ÚTILES

las cadenas (chains)   el destornillador (screwdriver)

el martillo (hammer)   la bomba de neumáticos (tire pump)

el gato (jack)   la llave de tuercas, simple (small wrench)

los alicates (pliers)   la llave de tuercas (monkey wrench)

Fill blanks with the Spanish term that identifies each tool.

1. Ésta es una _____

2. Éste es un _____

3. Ésta es una _____ (simple).

4. Éste es un _____

5. Éstos son unos _____

12-5 ¿QUÉ PASA CON MI COCHE? (Conversación)

A driver takes his car to a gasoline station because it has not been running well. After inspecting the automobile, the mechanic gives the driver a list of things that are wrong with it. Choose a partner and take on the roles of mechanic and owner. The mechanic will tell the owner what is wrong. The owner will ask questions or make a comment. Following are some suggestions. If you can improvise—fine!

Example:

El mecánico: La batería está débil. Necesita una nueva.
El motorista: ¿Por cuánto tiempo dura una batería?
El mecánico: Eso depende del uso.

¡ADELANTE!

El carburador (carburetor) está sucio.

La correa del ventilador (fan belt) está rota.

Las luces traseras no funcionan.

La rueda de recambio (spare tire) necesita aire.

El forro (brake lining) está gastado (worn).

El tubo de escape (exhaust pipe) tiene agujeros (holes).

El radiador tiene un agujero también.

El silenciador (muffler) no funciona bien.

El carro necesita lubricación.

El motorista: ¡Uf! ¡¡Yo necesito un carro nuevo!!

12-6 Señales de Carreteras

Listed below are road signs which should be noted. In the circles that follow each one, make a simple drawing that illustrates the printed words, as in the first example.

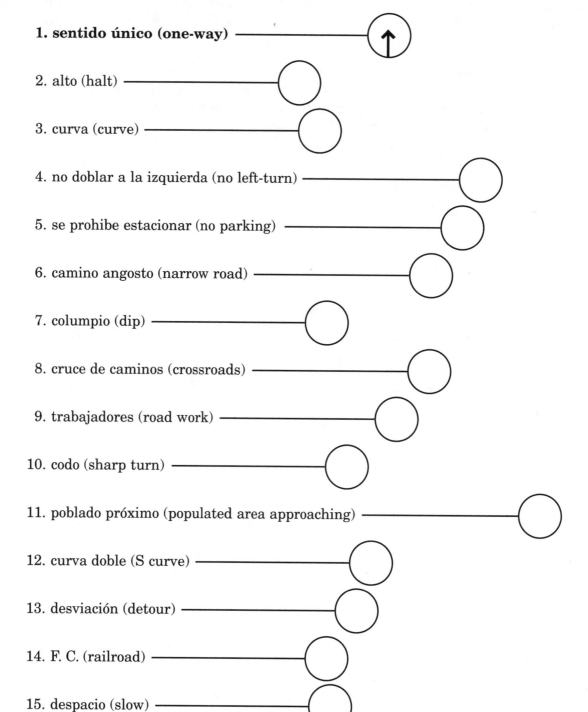

1. **sentido único (one-way)** ⬆
2. alto (halt)
3. curva (curve)
4. no doblar a la izquierda (no left-turn)
5. se prohibe estacionar (no parking)
6. camino angosto (narrow road)
7. columpio (dip)
8. cruce de caminos (crossroads)
9. trabajadores (road work)
10. codo (sharp turn)
11. poblado próximo (populated area approaching)
12. curva doble (S curve)
13. desviación (detour)
14. F. C. (railroad)
15. despacio (slow)
16. Modere su velocidad. (Lower your speed.)

Section 13

COMEMOS EN UN RESTAURANTE (DINING IN A RESTAURANT)

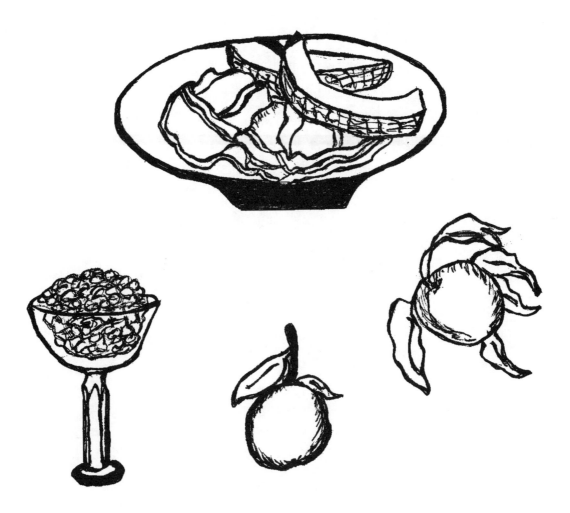

¡¡BUEN PROVECHO!!

¿A qué hora se come?	en un restaurante
platos típicos	el menú

13-1 FOOD NOTES (Background)

Spanish food is exotic and delicious. Some contains a great deal of olive oil and garlic, although in the better hotels and restaurants the food is mild and well-flavored.

The olive groves that dot the Spanish countryside were first planted by the Phoenicians, and the Romans used the olive oil in cooking. The Moors introduced saffron, widely used in Spanish cooking; it is the main condiment in the paella valenciana. Each region of Spain has its special dishes. The best known are:

el gazpacho	a vegetable soup originated by the Moors of Andalucía
la fabada	Asturian stew made of pork and beans
el cocido	boiled meat and vegetables, said to be of Jewish origin
la paella	rice, chicken, seafood, saffron; a specialty of Valencia
el pote gallego	a stew of beans, bacon, and vegetables

Breakfast is the usual Continental style—coffee, tea, or chocolate with a sweet roll. Lunch may start anywhere from 1:30 to 3:00 P.M. Because dinner-time is very late, lunch is the most substantial meal of the day. A siesta is generally taken after lunch. Some shops and places of business close for 2 1/2 hours, although this custom is waning. A "merienda" (snack) composed of "tapas," delicious tidbits, is taken at about 5:30 to 6:00 P.M. because dinner is not served until 9:00 or 10:00 P.M. or possibly later.

13-2 Un menú del restaurante "Buen Provecho"

APERITIVOS
coctel de frutas (fruit cocktail)

entremeses variados (hors d'oeuvres)

SOPAS
sopa de ajos (garlic soup)

sopa de verduras (vegetable soup)

sopa española: arroz, tomate, pimiento

CARNES
bistec a la parilla (grilled beefsteak)

chuletas de cerdo (pork chops)

chuletas de ternera (veal cutlets)

pata de cabrito (leg of goat)

pollo asado (roast chicken)

PESCADOS
calamares en su tinta (squid in its ink)

bacalao (codfish)

camarones en salsa verde (shrimp in green
    sauce)

ENSALADAS
ensalada de lechuga y tomate (lettuce and
    tomato salad)

ensalada de verduras (vegetable salad)

POSTRES
flan (custard)

helado de vainilla (vanilla ice cream)

queso y frutas frescas (cheese and fresh
    fruit)

BEBIDAS
café

té

leche (milk)

agua mineral

refrescos (sodas)

Use the menu to order a complete dinner in Spanish. Write your requests in complete sentences.

13-3 Diálogo: ¡No lo podemos creer!

Es sábado y son las dos de la tarde. El señor Gómez le pregunta a su esposa qué hay de comer.

Sra. G.:	Pues, tú sabes que hay muchas sobras los sábados, y para que no se echen a perder, siempre preparo un cocido.
Sr. G.:	No, no me apetece un cocido. Vamos a comer en el restaurante "Buen Provecho." ¡Tengo mucha hambre! (Entran en el restaurante. Hay una mesa desocupada, y se sientan. El camarero les da el menú.)
Sr. G.:	Tráigame un bistec, poco hecho, con papas fritas y una ensalada de verduras, por favor.
Sra. G.:	Yo estoy a régimen; quiero pollo asado y una ensalada de lechuga y tomate. (El camarero regresa después de unos minutos.)
Camarero:	Lo siento, pero no hay ni bistec ni pollo.
Sr. G.:	¿Hay camarones o pescado?
Camarero:	No, no hay más pescado.
Sra. G.:	¿Hay chuletas de cerdo?
Camarero:	No, señora, no hay más carne. Ustedes vinieron demasiado tarde para el almuerzo. Tenemos solamente la especialidad del día, pero tienen que esperar veinte minutos.
Sr. G.:	Está bien, ¡tráiganosla! (El camarero regresa con dos platos. Los pone delante de los clientes.)
Camarero:	Aquí está, nuestra rica especialidad—¡cocido! ¡Buen provecho!

Vocabulario

para que no se echen a perder (so that they don't spoil)

no me apetece. (It doesn't appeal to me.)

Tráigame (bring me)

poco hecho (rare)

a régimen (on a diet)

Lo siento (I'm sorry.)

la especialidad del día (the specialty of the day)

tráiganosla (Bring it to us.)

rica (delicious)

Complete usted las frases siguientes y dé las respuestas a las preguntas.

1. El señor Gómez le pregunta a su esposa _____

2. La señora responde que los sábados ella siempre hace _____

3. El señor Gómez le dice que _____

4. El señor Gómez quiere ir al _____

5. En el restaurante el señor Gómez pide _____

_____

6. El camarero les dice que _____

_____

7. El señor Gómez está muy _____

8. El camarero les dice que vinieron _____

_____

9. El camarero añade (adds) que _____

_____

10. Los señores Gómez dicen _____

11. Después de veinte minutos, ¿qué les trae el camarero? _____

_____

12. ¿Cree usted que el señor Gómez le debe dejar una propina (tip) al camarero?

Sí, porque _____

_____

No, porque _____

_____

_____

13-4 La palabra apropiada

Complete usted con la mejor palabra o expresión.

1. El _____ se come al final de la comida.

2. Una lista de platos es un _____ .

3. Un refresco es una _____ .

4. Una persona que sirve comidas en un restaurante es un (a) _____ .

5. Un restaurante tiene menos platos cuando uno llega _____ .

6. La paella es una especialidad de _____ .

7. El bacalao es un _____ .

8. En España la comida principal es el _____ .

9. Un coctel de frutas es un _____ .

10. Después de comer en un restaurante, el cliente deja una _____ .

11. La cena española se sirve desde las _____ .

12. El desayuno español consiste en _____ .

13-5 TRABALENGUAS

Practice this tongue twister for improving the pronunciation of the Spanish "rr" and "r."

Erre con erre, cigarro,

erre con erre, carril;

rápido corren los carros,

por los rieles del ferrocarril.

What in this picture starts with an "r," heavily trilled?

SHOPPING IN A DEPARTMENT STORE

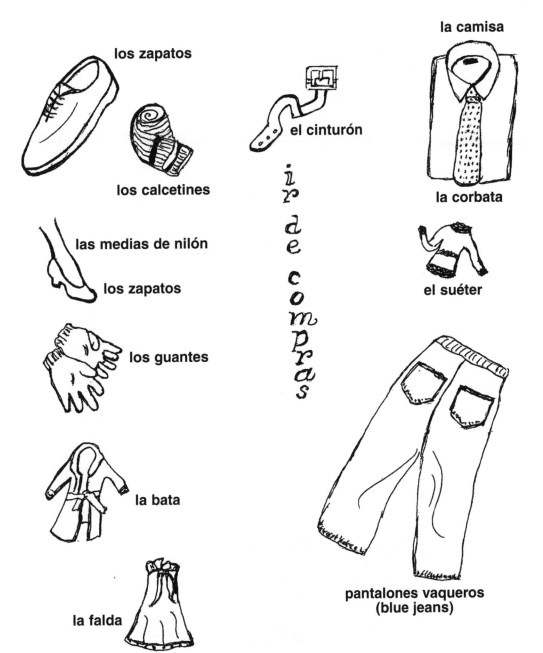

los zapatos

los calcetines

las medias de nilón

los zapatos

los guantes

la bata

la falda

el cinturón

ir de compras

la camisa

la corbata

el suéter

pantalones vaqueros
(blue jeans)

14-1 Diálogo: Se equivocó

El señor Melena quiere comprar un regalo para el cumpleaños de su esposa. Busca una tienda de artículos para señoras. ¿Qué compraré? se pregunta. Entra en la tienda.

Empleada:	Buenos días, señor. ¿En qué puedo servirle?
Sr. M.:	Pues, no sé, tal vez un par de guantes.
Empleada:	¿Guantes? ¿Para qué ocasión?
Sr. M.:	No sé.
Empleada:	¿De qué color?
Sr. M.:	No sé.
Empleada:	¿De seda o de algodón?
Sr. M.:	No sé. No importa.
Empleada:	¿De qué medida?
Sr. M.:	No sé.
	(La empleada está un poco nerviosa, pero trata de mantenerse calmada.)
Empleada:	Pues, aquí hay un bonito par de guantes de algodón, color canela, de talla mediana. (Piensa el señor M.: "No le hace. Mi esposa los cambiará," y regresando a casa le da los guantes a su esposa.)
La señora:	¡Qué sorpresa, querido! ¡Qué lindos! El color es igualito al color de mi vestido nuevo, y otra sorpresa—¡sabes mi medida! ¡Gracias!
Sr. M.:	No es nada. Me alegro de que te gusten.
	(Piensa: "¡Y yo creía que iba a cambiarlos!")

Vocabulario

Se equivocó (He was mistaken.)

el cumpleaños (birthday)

los guantes (gloves)

de seda (silk)

de algodón (cotton)

¿De qué medida? (What size?)

color canela (light brown)

la talla mediana (medium size)

No le hace. (It doesn't matter.)

igualito (exactly the same)

¡Qué esposo! (What a Husband!)

Dar respuestas a las preguntas siguientes.

1. ¿Cree usted que el señor Melena es una persona decisiva? _____

2. ¿Por qué no sabe las respuestas a las preguntas de la empleada? _____

   _____

3. ¿Cómo se comporta (behaves) la empleada? _____

4. ¿Por qué el regalo de su marido le sorprende a la esposa? _____

   _____

5. Además de no ser decisivo, ¿diría usted que el señor Melena es un mal hombre?

   _____

© 1996 by the Center for Applied Research in Education

14-2 LAS TIENDAS (THE STORES)

In Spain and some other Spanish-speaking countries, shops generally open from about 9:00 A.M. to 1:00 P.M. and from about 3:30 P.M. to 8:00 P.M. These hours may vary somewhat according to the season of the year. Sizes and measurements of clothing differ from those in use in the United States.

¿CÓMO SE DICE? (HOW DO YOU SAY. . . ?)

How much is it? (¿Cuánto es?)

It is too expensive. (Es demasiado caro.)

Do you have anything less expensive? (¿Tiene usted algo más barato?)

Will you accept a traveller's check? (¿Aceptará usted un cheque de viajero?)

Where can I find underwear? (¿Dónde encuentro ropa interior?)

Where are men's sweaters sold? (¿Dónde se venden suéteres para señores?)

What is the price of these shirts? (¿Qué precio tienen estas camisas?)

I'll take this one. (Me quedo con ésta.)

I don't know if I have enough money. (No sé si traigo bastante dinero.)

It's a real bargain. (Es una verdadera ganga.)

Do I pay here or at the cash register? (¿Pago aquí o a la caja?)

I want to go to the third floor. (Quiero ir al tercer piso.)

Where is the escalator? (¿Dónde está la escalera mecánica?)

I'd like to buy the blue umbrella that is in the display window. (Quisiera comprar el paraguas azul que está en el escaparate.)

¡COMPLÉTEME! (FILL IN THE PROPER WORDS.)

1. No tengo dinero contante (cash), solamente _____ .

2. Me gustan estos guantes pero son _____ .

3. ¿Tiene usted un par de guantes _____ ?

4. Quiero el vestido blanco que está en el _____ .

5. Mi marido necesita _____ .

6. ¿Están de venta (on sale) estos _____ ?

7. Está lloviendo; quiero comprar un _____ .

8. Quiero subir (go up) al cuarto piso. ¿Dónde está la _____ ?

9. ¿Pago a la _____ ?

10. Las _____ de la ropa son diferentes en España.

11. Las _____ se abren a las _____ de la mañana.

14-3 MÁS PRENDAS DE VESTIR
(MORE ARTICLES OF CLOTHING)

el abrigo	overcoat
la bata de baño	bathrobe
la blusa	blouse
la bufanda	scarf; head scarf
la camisa de vestir	dress shirt
la camiseta	undershirt
el camisón	nightgown
la chaqueta	jacket
la gorra de visera	peaked cap
el impermeable	raincoat
los pantalones	trousers
el pijama	pyjamas
el salto de cama	negligée; housecoat
el sombrero	hat
los trajes de deporte	sportswear
los trajes para caballeros	men's suits
las zapatillas	slippers
los zapatos de goma	rubbers

OTROS ARTÍCULOS (OTHER ARTICLES)

la bolsa	handbag
la cartera	wallet
las gafas	sunglasses
el pañuelo	handkerchief

KEEP IT LIVELY!

Divide into two groups. Group one calls out an article of clothing in Spanish or English.
Group two must give the equivalent in Spanish, if asked in English, and vice versa.

© 1996 by the Center for Applied Research in Education

14-4 MYSTERY WORD(S)

In the following word square there is one "lead" set of words that goes horizontally across the top, each letter of which starts a word that runs vertically. At the bottom of the square all the words are given in English. Write the Spanish equivalent of each. If you get them all right, the top, horizontal squares will spell the mystery word(s). A hint: the number of letters in each word is indicated by the number of vertical boxes.

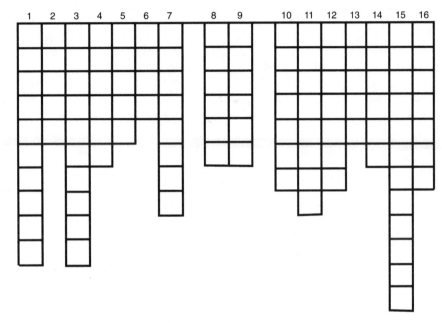

1. birthday

2. mood (cognate)

3. shop window

4. (he) wants

5. you (formal)

6. this (f.)

7. sweaters

8. money

9. husband

10. dress (noun)

11. exactly

12. cotton

13. (blue) trousers (same in both languages)

14. wife

15. underwear

16. an event (It's a cognate.)

Section 15

CONSULTAR AL DENTISTA
(CONSULTING A DENTIST)

Instrumentos del dentista

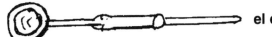 **el espejo (mirror) de boca**

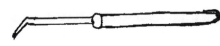 **el instrumento para la limpieza (cleaning) de dientes**

 **las tenazas (pliers) de extracción**

 **el mortero (mortar)**

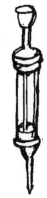 **la jeringa (syringe) hipodérmica para el anestésico local**

15-1 Diálogo: Tengo dolor de muela

Traduzca:

Carmen tiene la mejilla hinchada, cosa que le causa mucho dolor. Va al consultorio de su dentista, el doctor Sacamuelas.

Doctor S.: Hola, Carmencita. ¿Qué tienes en la boca, una manzana?

Carmen: No se burle de mí, doctor.* Tengo un dolor insoportable.

Doctor S.: Discúlpame. Veo que estás sufriendo. Siéntate aquí en el sillón; abre la boca y déjame ver las malas muelas.
(Después de examinar las muelas. . .)

Doctor S.: Tengo que sacar unos rayos X para ver qué hay debajo de los dos dientes. (El dentista comprueba que las dos muelas están picadas en el interior.)

Doctor S.: ¡Lo sospechaba! Las dos muelas están en malas condiciones. Puedo salvar una pero tengo que extraer la otra.

Carmen: ¿Va a dolerme mucho?

Doctor S.: No, solamente vas a sentir una picadura cuando te pongo una inyección de anestesia en la encía.
(Sin que Carmen pueda advertirlo, el dentista le ha extraído la mala muela.)

Doctor S.: ¡Aquí está la culpable de tu dolor!

Carmen: ¡Pues, no sentí nada!

Doctor S.: Bien. Te voy a dar estas pastillas por si tienes dolor más tarde. Ven a verme en tres días, y vamos a salvar la otra muela.

Carmen: Gracias, doctor. Parece que me siento mejor.

(Note: The dentist uses "tú" in addressing Carmen; she uses "usted" in addressing the dentist.)

Vocabulario

la mejilla hinchada (swollen cheek)

Discúlpame. (Forgive me.)

déjame ver (Let me see.)

sacar unos rayos X (to take some X-rays)

una inyección (an injection)

comprueba (proves)

picados (pitted with cavities)

una picadura (a prick)

la culpable (the guilty one)

insoportable (unbearable)

*Don't make fun of me, doctor.

15-2 ¡COMPLÉTEME!

Complete each sentence by filling in the blanks.

1. Carmen tiene _____ .

2. Carmen va a ver a _____ .

3. El dentista le pregunta a Carmen si tiene una _____ en la boca porque él

   nota que tiene la _____ .

4. Carmen se sienta en el _____ .

5. Primero, el dentista le _____ .

6. Luego, el dentista saca _____ .

7. Comprueba que las dos muelas _____ .

8. Él puede salvar _____ pero tiene que _____ la otra.

9. Cuando el dentista le sacó _____, Carmen no sintió (did not feel) ningún

   _____ .

10. El dentista le da algunas _____ por si tiene dolor _____ .

11. El dentista le dice a Carmen de volver a verlo en _____ .

12. Ahora que ya no tiene la muela _____ de su dolor, parece que

    Carmen se _____ .

© 1996 by the Center for Applied Research in Education

15-3 ¿QUÉ LE PASA?

On another sheet of paper, create ten sentences in Spanish using the terms below. Each sentence must include at least one of these terms but may use two or three.

Los dientes y la boca

los colmillos (eye teeth)

los caninos (canines)

las muelas (molars)

las muelas del juicio (wisdom teeth)

el paladar (roof of the mouth; palate)

las encías (gums)

la lengua (tongue)

la mandíbula (jaw)

los dientes de leche (milk teeth; first teeth)

los dientes permanentes (permanent teeth)

¿Qué puede pasar en la boca? (What can happen in the mouth?)

el absceso (abscess)

las caries (cavities)

la muela impactada (impacted tooth)

acumulación de sarro (accumulation of tartar)

la piorrea (pyorrhea [gum disease])

el tratamiento de canal (root canal treatment)

Para mantener la limpieza de los dientes usted debe usar:

el cepillo de dientes (toothbrush)

el hilo dental (dental floss)

la pasta de dientes (toothpaste) (also, pasta dentífrica)

el enjuague (mouthwash)

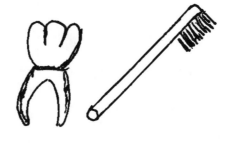

15-4 SEE WHO RATES THE HIGHEST
(25 = 100)

Questions 1 and 2 are worth five points each. You may answer these two questions in English. The blanks in the rest of the sentences—which you will fill in in Spanish—are worth one point each.

1. ¿Por qué ciertos dientes se llaman "dientes de juicio"? _____

_____

2. ¿Por qué ciertos dientes se llaman "caninos"? _____ 0

_____

3. ¿Cómo se llaman los primeros dientes del ser humano? _____

¿Y los que siguen? _____

4. Sin _____ no podemos hablar.

5. Los dientes crecen en _____ .

6. Las cosas más comunes que destruyen los dientes son _____ . La mayor parte de éstas se puede evitar usando el _____ y _____ después de cada comida, si es posible.

7. En el _____ el paciente se sienta en el _____ .

8. A veces es necesario _____ para ver dentro de una _____ .

9. Antes de _____ una muela, el dentista le da una _____ al paciente.

10. Una _____ puede causar una _____ .

© 1996 by the Center for Applied Research in Education

CONSULTAR AL MÉDICO
(CONSULTING A DOCTOR)

Parts of the Body
(Partes del cuerpo)

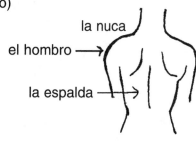

la nuca
el hombro →
la espalda →

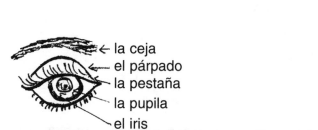

← la ceja
← el párpado
← la pestaña
← la pupila
← el iris

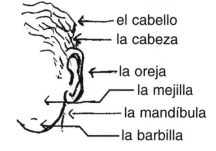

← el cabello
← la cabeza
← la oreja
— la mejilla
— la mandíbula
— la barbilla

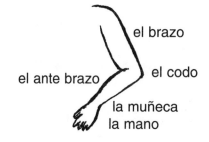

el brazo
el ante brazo · el codo
la muñeca
la mano

<u>la boca</u>
← los labios
los dientes

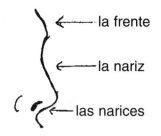

← la frente
← la nariz
← las narices

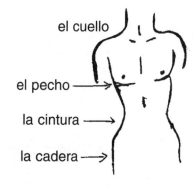

el cuello
el pecho →
la cintura →
la cadera →

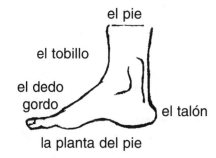

el pie
el tobillo
el dedo
gordo
el talón
la planta del pie

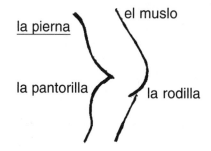

<u>la pierna</u>   el muslo
la pantorilla   la rodilla

16-1 PARTS OF THE BODY*

A few parts of the body can be spelled in English with three letters; for example, "eye." Write five of these parts in English and give their Spanish equivalents with their definite articles.

<u>ENGLISH</u>   <u>SPANISH</u>

1. _____   _____

2. _____   _____

3. _____   _____

4. _____   _____

5. _____   _____

List five parts of the body that you might have a problem with that could be helped by a doctor who specializes in sports medicine. Answer in English and in Spanish.

<u>ENGLISH</u>   <u>SPANISH</u>

6. _____   _____

7. _____   _____

8. _____   _____

9. _____   _____

10. _____   _____

© 1996 by the Center for Applied Research in Education

*Acknowledgement to Connie Kallback.

16-2 POINT... (A/B)

Play a Simon Says-type game. All students are on their feet. When the teacher calls out a part of the body (in Spanish), the students will point to it. Those who make a mistake or do not know where to point must sit down. The last one to remain standing is the winner.

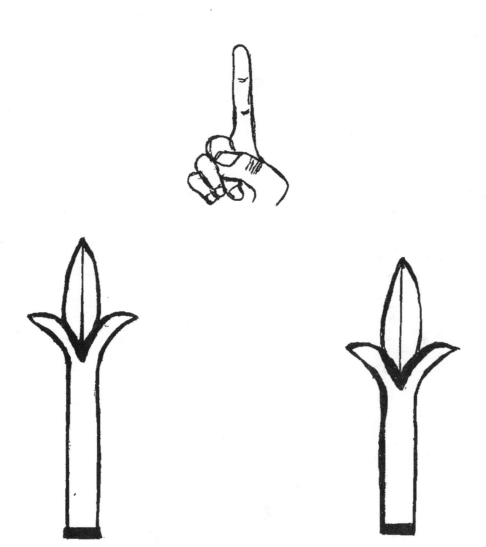

214

16-3 DIÁLOGO: PEQUEÑAS AMÍGDALAS, GRANDES PROBLEMAS

Traduzca:

Hace más de una semana que el señor Reyes tiene dolor de garganta. Por fin, decide consultar a su médico, el doctor Arias. El médico tiene puesta la bata blanca de médico y el estetoscopio al cuello.

Doctor A.:   Buenos días, señor Reyes. Hace mucho tiempo que no lo veo. ¿Qué le pasa?

Señor R.:   Pues, me duele mucho la garganta y cada día me resulta más difícil tragar.

Doctor A.:   Déjeme examinarle. Abra la boca; diga "ah." (El médico le examina la garganta, las orejas; le ausculta el pecho, y le toma la temperatura y la presión de la sangre.) ¿Desde cuándo tiene usted este dolor de garganta?

Señor R.:   Hace más de una semana. ¿Qué tengo, doctor?

Doctor A.:   Tiene las amígdalas muy inflamadas, un poco de congestión en los pulmones, y tiene fiebre. ¿Le duelen las coyunturas?

Señor R.:   Sí, eso también me molesta. ¿Qué se debe hacer, doctor?

Doctor A.:   Voy a recetarle un antibiótico para controlar la infección. Tome una pastilla cada cuatro horas, por una semana; luego quiero verle de nuevo. Pero la única solución es sacarle las amígdalas. Si no, este problema va a volver a molestarle.

Señor R.:   Gracias, doctor. Eso de la operación lo voy a pensar. Por el momento mi trabajo no me lo permite.

Doctor A.:   Entonces, hasta luego. ¡Qué se mejore pronto!

En el consultorio del médico hay un botiquín que contiene:

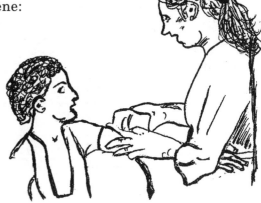

el alcohol para frotar (rubbing alcohol)

el algodón (absorbent cotton)

la curita (Band-Aid)

el vendaje (bandage)

el yodo (iodine)

el termómetro (thermometer)

los guantes de goma (rubber gloves)

VOCABULARIO

Me duele la garganta. (I have a sore throat.)

tragar (to swallow)

las amígdalas inflamadas (diseased tonsils)

los pulmones (lungs)

ausculta (auscultar) (listen to through a stethoscope; auscultate)

la fiebre (fever)

la pastilla (tablet)

¡Qué se mejore pronto! (May you feel better soon.)

16-4 ¡BÚSQUEME Y TRADÚZCAME!

The word square contains medical expressions used in the dialogue in 16-3. They are in English. Find them, circle them, and write the Spanish equivalent at the bottom of the square. Include the definite article of the nouns.

The words may be horizontal, vertical, diagonal, or in reverse order.

A	L	M	N	O	I	T	S	E	G	N	O	C
U	S	T	M	N	O	I	T	C	E	F	N	I
S	E	L	E	T	U	S	L	I	S	N	O	T
C	N	U	L	X	O		M	S	Q	O	V	O
U	I	S	B	O			A	B	T	R	I	
L	M	N	O	V	O		N	R	T	O	E	B
T	A	O	R	H	T	F	G	L	T	U	V	I
A	X	C	P	A	I	N	V	C	R	S	E	T
T	E	L	B	A	T	S	O	G	H	I	F	N
E	M	O	U	T	H	D	L	U	N	G	S	A
M	E	R	U	T	A	R	E	P	M	E	T	I

_____   _____

_____   _____

_____   _____

_____   _____

_____   _____

_____   _____

_____   _____

_____   _____

_____   _____

_____   _____

_____   _____

_____   _____

_____   _____

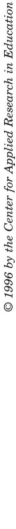

16-5 ENFERMEDADES

Using the terms from this list, create five sentences in Spanish. Use the lines at the bottom of the page.

la acidez	acidity	los escalofríos	chills
el agotamiento	exhaustion	el estreñimiento	constipation
la alergia	allergy	la gripe	flu
la ampolla	blister	la hemorragia	hemorrhage
el ardor de estómago	heartburn	la hinchazón	swelling
la bronquitis	bronchitis	la indigestión	indigestion
el calambre	cramp	el mareo	dizziness
el catarro	cold	el reumatismo	rheumatism
el coágulo de sangre	bloodclot	la tos	cough
el desmayo	fainting spell	el virus	virus
el dolor agudo	sharp pain		

1. _____

_____

2. _____

_____

3. _____

_____

4. _____

_____

5. _____

_____

16-6 ¡COMPLÉTEME!

En el espacio en blanco escriba usted la palabra apropiada, la primera letra de la cual está dada.

1. Después de comer frutas agrias (sour), sufro de a_____ .

2. El paciente tuvo una h_____ ; el médico le dio una transfusión de sangre.

3. La señora Montoya llamó la ambulancia porque su marido tenía

   d_____ en el pecho.

4. El paciente tenía un c_____ .

5. El nadador (swimmer) sufrió un c_____ y se ahogó (drowned).

6. "No comas tanto, querido; no quiero que sufras un ataque de i_____."

7. Una inflamación en los bronquios causa la b_____ .

8. Si no se cuida el c_____ , puede convertirse en g_____ .

9. Mi abuela no puede caminar porque tiene r_____ .

10. Los rayos del sol pueden causar a_____ en las espaldas.

11. La caída (fall) le dio una h_____ en la frente.

12. Cuando no sabemos qué nos hace sentir mal, decimos que tenemos el

    v_____ .

© 1996 by the Center for Applied Research in Education

16-7 DIÁLOGO: ¿TV O NO TV?—ES LA PREGUNTA

Paciente: Doctor, tengo frecuentes dolores de cabeza y, a veces, jaquecas (migrañas) por mirar la televisión demasiado. ¿Puede usted recetar algún remedio?

Médico: ¿Cuántas horas al día pasa usted en frente del aparato?

Paciente: Pues, una hora antes de ir a mi trabajo y seis horas al regresar. El fin de semana mi esposa se llama "viuda de televisionista," y se enoja.

Médico: Pues, yo le diría de mirar la tele menos horas. Si no, usted va a tener jaquecas provenientes de problemas familiares.

VOCABULARIO

jaquecas (migraines)

se enoja (becomes annoyed)

yo le diría (I would tell you.)

provenientes (stemming from)

¿TELEVISIÓN—MÁS O MENOS?

Answer the following questions.

1. ¿Por cuántas horas al día mira usted la televisión? _____ .

2. ¿Padece usted de los ojos? (Do you suffer from eyestrain?) _____ .

3. ¿Cree usted que mirar la televisión por siete horas al día es demasiado? _____ .

4. ¿Cree usted que tiene razón en enojarse la esposa cuando su marido no hace nada durante el fin de semana sino mirar la televisión? _____ .

5. (a) ¿Prefiere usted mirar la televisión por muchas horas y tener jaquecas? _____ .

   (b) ¿Prefiere usted mirar la televisión por menos horas y no tener jaquecas? _____ .

6. ¿Cuál es su programa favorito? _____

   _____ .

Don't be a "couch potato."
Be selective in your TV viewing.

16-8 Ouch!

Unscramble the following illnesses* in Spanish. Give the English equivalent in the second column. Then put together the circled letters which will spell a discomfort that some swimmers experience. What is it?

1. la geríala _____ _____

2. la sto _____ _____

3. el breamcal _____ _____

4. la egpri _____ _____

5. el ñbao _____ _____

6. la quitisbron _____ _____

7. el yamosed _____ _____

8. la zedcia _____ _____

9. el meora _____ _____

10. la nózahcnih _____ _____

11. el omsitamuer _____ _____

12. el rolod _____ _____

Las letras con círculos: _ _ _ _ _ _ _ _ _

La palabra es: _____

© 1996 by the Center for Applied Research in Education

* There is one exception.

DEPORTES (SPORTS)

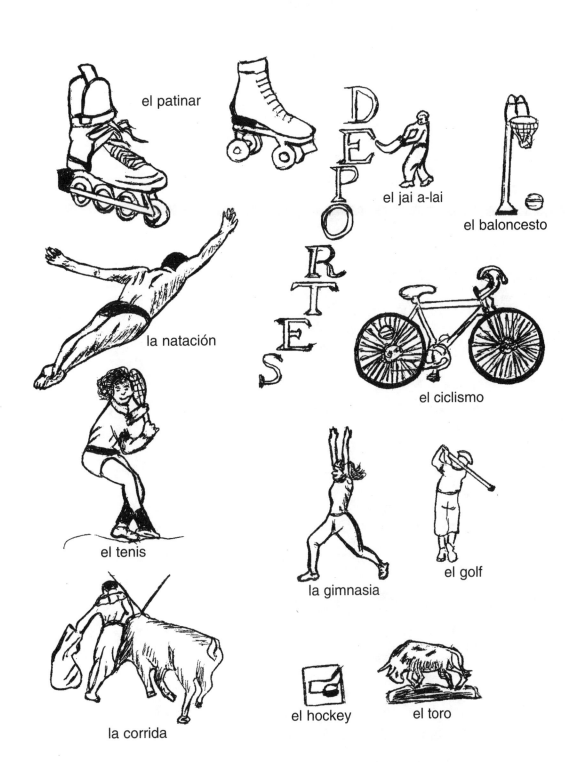

el patinar

DEPORTES

el jai a-lai

el baloncesto

la natación

el ciclismo

el tenis

la gimnasia

el golf

la corrida

el hockey

el toro

17-1 DEPORTES (SPORTS)

patinar en hielo

Sports, a healthful form of physical exercise, have an interesting history. The Greeks participated in a series of sports that are still practiced in the Olympics. In medieval times military maneuvers were the main sports activity. Today the field of sports is highly organized throughout the world and is a very profitable business that entertains millions.

el boxeo

la pelota de béisbol

Directions:

From the descriptions of various sports that follow, select your favorites and translate the Spanish into English on a separate sheet. In most sports both men and women participate.

el guante de boxeo

el bate de béisbol

1. <u>El jai a-lai</u> (Basque ball game, similar to handball). El nombre quiere decir (means) "fiesta alegre." Se usa un cesto (basket) atado al brazo (attached to the arm) para coger y tirar la pelota. Es un juego popular en los países hispanoamericanos, especialmente en Cuba, México, Venezuela, y por supuesto–España. Hay dos equipos (teams); cada uno consta de un delantero (forward) y de un zaguero (back). Es un juego rápido, brusco (tough) y peligroso. Las canchas (courts) tienen tres muros hechos de cemento sólido. El muro se llama "frontón." El jugador tira la pelota contra el frontón.

el guante de béisbol

el balón de fútbol

2. <u>El tenis</u> (tennis). Se envía una pelota por encima de una red (net) horizontal. Hay dos o cuatro jugadores (hombres o mujeres) que forman dos campos (sides). Se usan raquetas y pelotas de tenis. Hay un árbitro (umpire) y un recogedor de pelotas (one who picks up and replaces the tennis balls). Es más popular que nunca en los países hispanos porque hay muchos jugadores sobresalientes (outstanding) de origen hispanoamericano.

el esquiar

el béisbol

el pescar

3. <u>El vólibol, balonvolea</u> (volleyball). Hay dos equipos (teams) separados por una red horizontal. Generalmente tiene lugar (takes place) en un gimnasio. Cada jugador(a) trata de echar con la mano un balón por encima de la red en el campo opuesto antes de que toque el suelo. Se juega principalmente en barrios (neighborhoods) y parques. Es popular en México, Cuba, Bolivia y Colombia.

4. <u>El béisbol.</u> Hay nueve jugadores en cada campo. Se usan una pelota y un bate (bat). El equipo consta de, entre otros, un receptor (catcher), un lanzador (pitcher), un bateador (batter). En el diamante (diamond)—campo de juego (field)—hay tres bases: la primera base (first base), la segunda base (second base) y la tercera base (third base). También hay el cuadro del bateador (batter's box) y la plataforma de lanzamiento (pitcher's mound). Es un deporte muy popular en Cuba, Puerto Rico, la República Dominicana, Venezuela, Panamá, Nicaragua y México.

5. <u>El básquetbol, el baloncesto</u> (basketball). Hay cinco jugadores por cada bando (side). El juego consiste en tirar (throw) el balón (basketball) en un cesto (basket) colocado a cierta altura (placed at a certain height), en frente del cual hay una línea de los tiros libres (free throws).

6. <u>El fútbol</u> (lo que se llama *soccer* en los Estados Unidos) es rey en los países hispánicos. Un equipo tiene once jugadores y consta de, entre otros, el centro (center), el defensa (fullback) y el medio (halfback). El campo de fútbol es más grande que un campo de fútbol americano. El juego consiste en hacer entrar la pelota en la portería (goal) del equipo contrario. Los aficionados exclaman:

> ¡Van a hacer un pase! (They're going to pass!)
>
> ¡Vaya un choque! (What a collision!)
>
> ¡Es un empate! (It's a tie!)

7. <u>El boxeo</u> es un deporte de combate. Se usan guantes especiales con los cuales se dan puñetazos (punches) hasta que uno de los dos triunfe (wins). Para entrenarse (train) los boxeadores tienen compañeros de entrenamiento (sparring partners). Practican con el balón (punching bag). En el cerrado (ring) tratan de no dar golpes bajos (to hit below the belt), o meterse al cuerpo a cuerpo (clinch) con su adversario. Tratan de dar el golpe de abajo arriba (uppercut). Cuando suena el *gong*, los dos boxeadores tienen que irse al ángulo neutral (neutral corner). Uno de ellos puede ser derrotado (defeated) por fuera de combate (knockout).

© 1996 by the Center for Applied Research in Education

el cuadrilátero de boxeo

17-1 DEPORTES (SPORTS) *(continued)*

8. <u>El golf</u> es un juego que consiste en enviar una pelota con un palo (club) en una serie de agujeros (holes) (9 o 18) en terreno accidentado (uneven surface) y cubierto de césped (grass). El jugador empieza con la salida (tee). Cuando está cerca de un agujero hace un tiro al hoyo (putt). Generalmente el jugador tiene que tener cuidado (must be careful) con los obstáculos. El jugador de golf tiene un portador de palos de golf (caddie).

9. <u>La natación</u> (swimming). Para principiantes (beginners) se nada en una piscina (pool) usando una almohada flotadora (floating pillow) o un cinturón de corcho (cork belt). Se aprende a hacer la braza de pecho (breast stroke) y la braza de mariposa (butterfly stroke).

10. <u>Jugar a las bochas</u> (bowl). Se ponen nueve bolos (ninepins) en una bolera (alley). Con una bola el jugador trata de derribar (knock down) los que pueda.

11. Hay otros deportes populares:

> esquiar (skiing)
>
> patinar en hielo (ice skating)
>
> pescar (fishing) (Se usan redes [nets] o cañas [fishing poles] para sacar peces del agua.)
>
> caminar (walking) (Se sigue un curso a pie.)
>
> ciclismo (cycling) (Es un deporte de los aficionados a la bicicleta.)
>
> montar a caballo (horseback riding)
>
> andar a trote corto (jogging)
>
> gimnasia (gymnastics)

17-2 IDENTIFIQUE USTED EL DEPORTE (IDENTIFY THE SPORT)

El ejercicio es el principio vital de la salud.
James Thompson
(1700–1748)

Give the name of the sport for each picture shown below. Also give a complete translation of the object.

el patinaje de figuras

1. _____

raqueta de tenis

2. _____

red de tenis

3. _____

zapatos de patinar

4. _____

montar a caballo

5. _____

casco

6. _____

bolas

7. _____

la bolera (la cancha de bochas)

8. _____

17-3 ¡BÚSQUEME—EN ESPAÑOL!

Find the following sports given in Spanish in the word square and circle each one. They can be horizontal or vertical. Definite articles are not used in the word square.

1. gymnastics	7. basketball	13. baseball
2. volleyball	8. jogging	14. skiing
3. bicycling	9. soccer	15. bullfighting
4. golf	10. hockey	16. swimming
5. bowling	11. ice skating	17. fishing
6. walking	12. boxing	18. handball

¡Déme el número correspondiente en inglés!

Write the number of the English sport which corresponds with the Spanish sport listed below:

© 1996 by the Center for Applied Research in Education

(Example) **la corrida**	15
el jai a-lai	18
la natación	___
la gimnasia	___
el pescar	___
el esquiar	___
el béisbol	___
el patinar en hielo	___
el boxeo	___
el golf	___
el ciclismo	___
el hockey	___
el vólibol	___
el fútbol	___
el baloncesto	___
jugar a las bochas	___
caminar	___
andar a trote corto	___
el básquetbol	___

B	S	O	S	V	O	L	I	B	O	L	B	P	O	M	B
A	A	M	O	O	T	E	N	O	A	O	A	A	S	O	A
S	L	C	N	F	H	S	D	X	T	M	I	T	O	N	L
Q	I	I	R	U	E	Q	Y	E	E	A	L	I	N	E	O
U	R	C	I	T	O	U	R	O	Z	E	O	N	A	D	N
E	D	L	S	B	R	I	A	U	T	O	N	A	N	A	C
T	E	I	A	O	I	A	P	E	S	C	A	R	A	D	E
B	A	S	I	L	A	R	R	L	O	M	N	E	D	E	S
O	R	M	V	W	X	H	O	C	K	E	Y	N	A	O	T
L	M	O	S	C	A	M	I	N	A	R	O	H	R	R	O
B	A	I	L	E	J	A	I	A	L	A	I	I	N	G	E
B	E	I	S	B	O	L	D	E	J	A	R	E	N	O	X
A	L	M	A	C	O	R	R	I	D	A	P	L	I	L	T
J	U	G	A	R	A	B	O	C	H	A	S	O	L	F	R
A	N	D	A	R	A	T	R	O	T	E	C	O	R	T	O
H	A	C	E	R	G	I	M	N	A	S	I	A	S	I	L

17-4 ¡JUGUEMOS! (LET'S PLAY)

(1) En este cuadro hay los nombres de diez deportes. Están puestos horizontalmente, por la derecha o al revés. Haga un círculo en cada uno de ellos, y (2) complete la frase, según el primer ejemplo. (3) En cada dos líneas del cuadro hay parte de una frase que describe los deportes. ¡Descífrela!

(1)	L	P	A	T	I	N	A	R	E	N	H	I	E	L	O
	W	X	O	P	L	O	S	D	E	P	O	R	T	E	S
(2)	N	S	T	I	A	L	A	I	A	J	R	P	Q	U	T
	S	O	N	E	J	E	R	C	I	C	I	O	S	A	M
(3)	A	M	B	A	L	O	N	C	E	S	T	O	C	O	N
	R	U	M	B	A	A	L	F	I	S	I	C	O	S	S
(4)	V	E	R	D	E	F	L	O	G	A	R	P	I	S	A
	A	L	I	M	E	N	T	O	S	Q	U	E	S	O	N
(5)	E	F	Ū	T	B	O	L	V	A	M	P	I	R	E	N
	S	A	L	U	D	A	B	L	E	S	Y	C	O	N	E
(6)	M	E	L	E	N	A	B	E	I	S	B	O	L	O	S
	A	S	A	P	A	R	A	N	I	Ñ	O	S	E	L	L
(7)	I	S	I	N	E	T	M	A	N	O	L	O	U	N	D
	Y	N	I	N	A	S	W	A	X	I	N	G	L	O	O
(8)	T	R	A	E	X	O	B	M	A	N	I	O	B	R	A
	V	O	C	A	C	I	O	N	H	O	M	B	R	E	S
(9)	C	O	M	O	E	S	X	C	I	C	L	I	S	M	O
	Y	M	U	J	E	R	E	S	B	I	L	L	E	T	O
(10)	G	L	A	M	O	L	O	B	I	L	O	V	E	N	D

(1) ¡DÉME UN CÍRCULO!*

1. Para
2. Para jugar al
3. Para jugar al
4. Para jugar al
5. Para jugar al
6. Para jugar al
7. Para jugar al
8. Para
9. Para el
10. Para jugar al

(2) ¿QUÉ SE NECESITA?

se necesitan   botas atadas a patines.

se necesitan   _____

se necesitan   _____

se necesitan   _____

se necesitan   _____

se necesitan   _____

se necesitan   _____

se necesitan   _____

se necesitan   _____

se necesitan   _____

(3) ¡DESCÍFREME! _____ .

* The numbers that follow coincide with those to the left of the square

17-5 DEPORTES

Traduzca:

Hay muchos aficionados (fans) de deportes en los países hispanos. Además del campo deportivo general, hay dos deportes que son típicamente españoles—la corrida (the bullfight) y el jai a-lai, un deporte vasco similar al juego de pelota.

Todos los domingos hay corridas en México y en España. También son populares en el Perú y en Colombia. La corrida de toros empieza a las cuatro en punto. El desfile de la cuadrilla (the parade of the bullfighters) en la plaza de toros es un espectáculo excitante. El "traje de luces" (the suit of lights) que lleva el torero es bordado con hilo de oro y de plata. En el desfile hay los siguientes participantes:

  el matador (kills the bull)

  el picador (mounted bullfighter who wounds the bull with a pike)

  el capeador ("plays" the bull with a cape)

A veces uno de ellos recibe cornadas (gorings) del toro.

El torero principal tiene una muleta en la mano—un palo que lleva pendiente un paño, generalmente rojo, que sirve para provocar al toro y hacerle bajar la cabeza cuando va a matarlo.

Hay dos fuerzas que se oponen aquí, la fuerza brutal de un animal enfurecido contra la valentía y la gracia del hombre.

El torero es un héroe nacional en España y en México. Para apreciar la corrida tenemos que comprender el arte y la destreza del torero.

ANSWER KEY

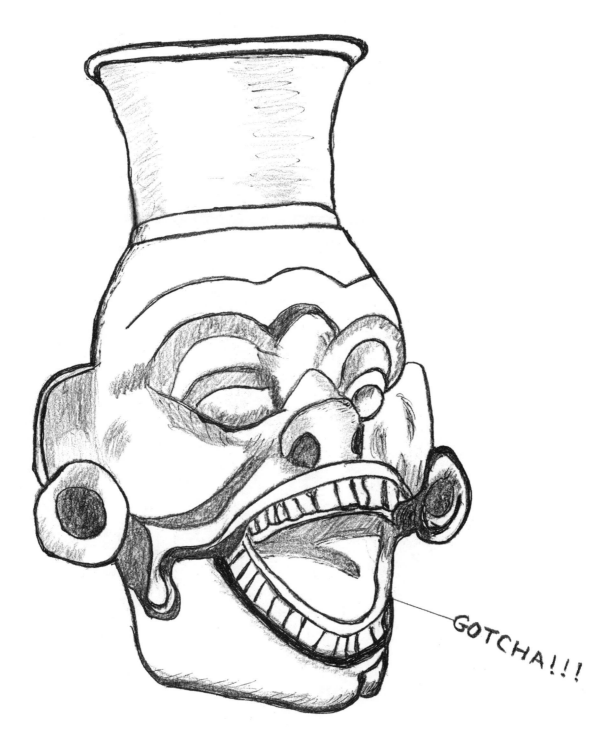

GOTCHA!!!

Section 1: LANGUAGE AND GEOGRAPHIC CHARACTERISTICS

1-5 RIVERS AND CITIES OF SPAIN

1. Ebro
2. Tajo
3. Duero
4. Guadiana
5. Guadalquivir
6. Barcelona
7. Bilbao
8. Burgos
9. Cádiz
10. Córdoba
11. Granada
12. Madrid
13. Salamanca
14. Santiago de Compostela
15. Sevilla
16. Toledo
17. Valencia

Note: In 1 through 5, those names with the same number of letters may vary in order.

1-6 PAÍSES DE HABLA-ESPAÑOLA

alba (n., dawn)
años (n., years)
apio (n., celery)
aspa (n., crosspiece)
alas (n., wings)
beso (n., kiss)
bola (n., globe)
bala (n., bullet)
base (n., basis)
baña (v., he bathes, "bañar")
baño (n., bath)
debe (v., owes, "deber")
debo (v., I owe, "deber")
daba (v., used to give, "dar")
días (n., days)
daño (n., danger)
dios (n., god)
esos (adj., m., those)
esas (adj., f., those)
hada (n., fairy)
hola (inter., hello)
haba (n., bean)
hiel (n., bile)

isla (n., island)
idea (n., idea)
idas (n., goings)
ibas (v., you used to go. "ir")
leño (n., wood)
leas (v., subjunctive, you read, "leer")
losa (n., slab)
lobo (n., wolf)
líos (n., messes)
leal (adj., m., f., loyal)
liso (adj., m., smooth)
lado (n., side)
osas (n., she-bears)
olas (n., waves)
piso (n., floor)
peña (n., rock)
pase (v., subjunctive, pass, "pasar")
pesa (v., weighs, "pesar")
plan (n., plan)
pila (n., basin)
pasa (v., passes, "pasar")

paso (n., step)
palo (n., pole)
paño (n., cloth)
polo (n., polo-sport)
papá (n., papa)
piña (n., pine cone)
seas (v., subjunctive, you are, "ser")
sola (adj., f., alone)
sapo (n., toad)
sois (v., you [vosotros] are, "ser")
seda (n., silk)
seña (n., sign)
sepa (v., subjunctive, know, "saber")
seso (n., brain)
sabe (v., knows, "saber")
sala (n., room)
saña (n., rage)
silo (n., cave)
sopa (n., soup)
soda (n., soda)
sana (v., heals, "sanar")

1-7 FIND THE ERRORS

1. No. El Amazonas
2. No. Sudamérica
3. No. Cataluña
4. Sí.
5. No. El Mediterráneo
6. No. quince (1492)
7. No. El Golfo de México
8. No. diez y siete
9. Sí.
10. Sí.
11. Sí.
12. No. México
13. No. El Tajo
14. No. El Uruguay
15. Sí.

1-8 EIGHT STRAIGHT; ONE SCRAMBLED

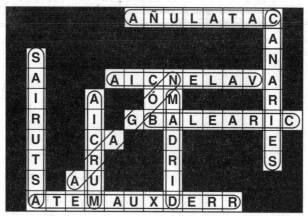

Aragón	Balearic
Madrid	Canaries
Murcia	Cataluña
Asturias	Valencia
Scrambled name:	Extremadura

(See 1-4 for a listing of 17 autonomous regions of Spain.)

1-9 SPANISH-SPEAKING COUNTRIES AND THEIR CAPITALS

1. Argentina (Buenos Aires)
2. Bolivia (La Paz)
3. Chile (Santiago)
4. Colombia (Bogotá)
5. Costa Rica (San José)
6. Cuba (Havana)
7. Ecuador (Quito)
8. El Salvador (San Salvador)
9. España (Madrid)
10. Guatemala (Guatemala City)
11. Honduras (Tegucigalpa)
12. México (México, Distrito Federal)
13. Nicaragua (Managua)
14. Panamá (Panama City)
15. Paraguay (Asunción)
16. Perú (Lima)
17. Puerto Rico (San Juan)
18. República Dominicana (Santo Domingo)
19. Uruguay (Montevideo)
20. Venezuela (Caracas)

© 1996 by the Center for Applied Research in Education

1-10 ALL BEGINNING WITH "AL..."

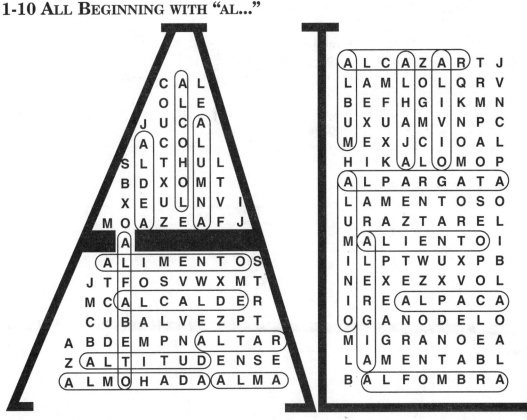

1. almohada (f.) pillow
2. alpargata (f.) hemp sandal
3. aluminio (m.) aluminum
4. alcázar (m.) fortress
5. alfombra (f.) carpet
6. altitud (f.) altitude
7. alimento (m.) food
8. alcalde (m., f.) mayor
9. alergia (f.) allergy
10. alfabeto (m.) alphabet
11. alhaja (f.) jewel
12. aliento (m.) breath
13. alivio (m.) relief
14. alma (f.) soul
15. aldea (f.) village
16. alcohol (m.) alcohol
17. álbum (m.) album
18. alpaca (f.) alpaca (wool)
19. altar (m.) altar
20. alumna/o (f., m.) student

Section 2: COGNATES

2-1 RECOGNIZING COGNATES

Yesterday a <u>horrible</u> <u>accident</u> <u>occurred</u>. My brother was driving his car in the city. He is a very <u>competent</u> and careful driver (<u>chauffeur</u>). Suddenly another <u>automobile</u> passed the red light and collided with my brother's <u>vehicle</u>. The <u>policeman</u> came; asked for the <u>documentation</u> of both drivers (<u>conductors</u>). The <u>imprudent</u> one had no insurance <u>policy</u> nor any other <u>necessary</u> <u>documents</u>. It turned out that his <u>auto</u> was stolen. Therefore, the <u>perpetrator</u> was taken to <u>prison</u> and my brother was taken to the <u>hospital</u> because he suffered a <u>nervous</u> <u>prostration</u>.

2-3 TRANSLATE: COGNATES ENDING IN "-CTO"

1. <u>act</u>; <u>defect:</u> El primer acto del drama tenía un defecto.
2. <u>intellect:</u> Albert Einstein tenía un gran intelecto.
3. <u>product:</u> La novela *Don Quijote de la Mancha* es el producto de un maestro en sátira, Miguel de Cervantes.
4. <u>aspect:</u> El actor tenía un aspecto feroz.
   <u>effect:</u> El efecto sobre su víctima era espantoso.
5. <u>contact:</u> El piloto perdió todo contacto con el campo de aviación.

2-4 "-CTO" ENDINGS

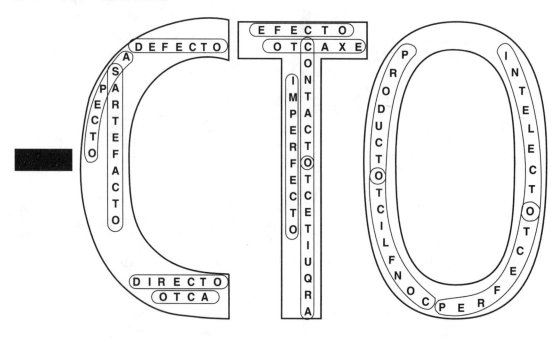

1. acto (act)	8. directo (direct)
2. arquitecto (architect)	9. efecto (effect)
3. artefacto (artefact)	10. exacto (exact)
4. aspecto (aspect)	11. imperfecto (imperfect)
5. conflicto (conflict)	12. intelecto (intellect)
6. contacto (contact)	13. perfecto (perfect)
7. defecto (defect)	14. producto (product)

2-5 TRANSLATE: "-IST" ENDINGS

1. El capitalista es una persona que tiene mucho dinero.
2. Un(a) turista viaja por todo el mundo.
3. Un(a) optimista dice que el vaso está medio lleno.
4. Un(a) pesimista dice que está medio vacío.
5. Alicia De Larrocha es una gran pianista.
6. Anton Rubinstein era un gran pianista y compositor.
7. Un(a) idealista lo ve todo color de rosa.
8. Diego Velásquez es un sobresaliente artista español.

2-6 "One Who" : Word Puzzle

```
I N D I V I D U A L I S T A
N   E   C O M U N I S T A   T
D   N A A     A N A E   T S
U A T T   A T G T C S I
T I S T   U U S O I T
S S I I   S R I N N R
R I T L   I A S F O I E
I S A R U L T I M L C
A E L A C A I A C I O N
L R E F O R M I S T A S I O
I G       C T P T V C
S N       O A     A
T O R G A N I S T A
A C T I V I S T A T S I E D
```

1. dentista
2. oculista
3. economista
4. comunista
5. socialista
6. organista
7. pacifista
8. violinista
9. deísta
10. concertista
11. congresista
12. reformista
13. lingüista
14. industrialista
15. individualista
16. activista
17. naturalista
18. artista

2-7 Translate: From "-ty" to "-dad"

1. La realidad del crimen era horrible.
2. Los gatos tienen mucha curiosidad.
3. Benjamin Franklin usó un cometa para probar que había electricidad en los relámpagos.
4. Dicen que la variedad es la sazón de la vida.
5. La velocidad del tren causó el accidente.

2-8 Spanish Cognates for "-ity" Endings

1. authority — autoridad
2. credibility — credibilidad
3. complexity — complexidad
4. culpability — culpabilidad
5. anxiety — ansiedad
6. felicity — felicidad
7. improbability — improbabilidad
8. impartiality — imparcialidad
9. insincerity — insinceridad
10. nationality — nacionalidad
11. maternity — maternidad
12. necessity — necesidad
13. opportunity — oportunidad
14. personality — personalidad
15. probability — probabilidad
16. stability — estabilidad *

*A Spanish word never starts with "s" followed by a consonant. The "s" is preceded by an "e," unless the "s" is followed by a vowel: sano, senador, sincero, pero "especial."

237

2-9 Buscapalabras: "-dad" Words

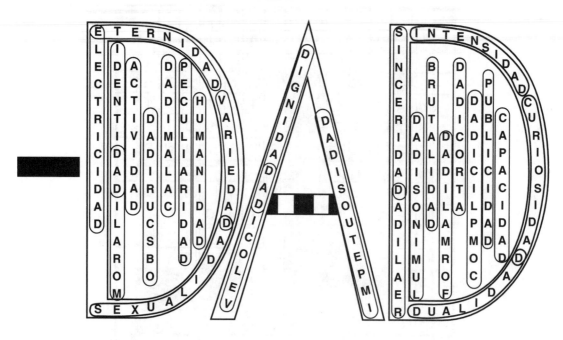

actividad (activity)
atrocidad (atrocity)
brutalidad (brutality)
calamidad (calamity)
capacidad (capacity)
complicidad (complicity)
curiosidad (curiosity)
dignidad (dignity)
dualidad (duality)
electricidad (electricity)
eternidad (eternity)
formalidad (formality)
humanidad (humanity)

identidad (identity)
impetuosidad (impetuosity)
intensidad (intensity)
luminosidad (luminosity)
moralidad (morality)
obscuridad (obscurity)
peculiaridad (peculiarity)
publicidad (publicity)
realidad (reality)
sexualidad (sexuality)
sinceridad (sincerity)
variedad (variety)
velocidad (velocity)

2-10 "-tion" Cognates

1. acción
2. ambición
3. atención
4. celebración
5. condición

6. descripción
7. elección
8. emoción
9. intención
10. revolución

Fill in the Blanks

11. atención
12. celebración
13. descripción
14. ambición
15. condición

16. acción
17. elección
18. revolución
19. emoción
20. intención

© 1996 by the Center for Applied Research in Education

2-11 A Prize for the Most! ("-ción" Cognates)

amputation (amputación)
collaboration (colaboración)
communication (comunicación)
compensation (compensación)
confederation (confederación)
consideration (consideración)
construction (construcción)
contamination (contaminación)
contrition (contrición)
destruction (destrucción)
elaboration (elaboración)

evacuation (evacuación)
evaluation (evaluación)
function (función)
generation (generación)
indication (indicación)
instruction (instrucción)
locomotion (locomoción)
lubrication (lubricación)
mention (mención)
nation (nación)
operation (operación)

2-12 "-ce" Endings to "-cia"

ambulancia
audiencia
cadencia
competencia
conferencia
continencia
correspondencia

diligencia
distancia
elegancia
eminencia
excelencia
existencia
independencia

inocencia
inteligencia
insignificancia
paciencia
presencia
prudencia

2-13 Turn Around: Spanish into English

1. continence
2. correspondence
3. difference
4. elegance
5. eminence
6. essence
7. excellence
8. existence
9. experience
10. insignificance
11. jurisprudence
12. magnificence
13. malevolence
14. patience
15. presence
16. prudence

2-14 Buscapalabras: Find the Mystery Word!

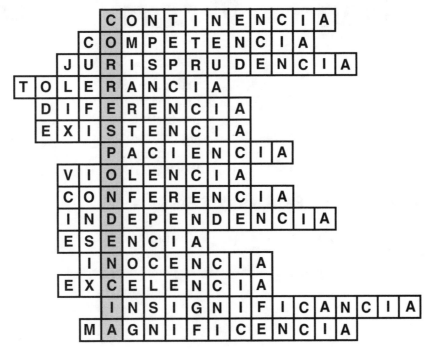

239

2-15 ADJECTIVE TO ADJECTIVE

1. active
2. attractive
3. constructive
4. descriptive
5. diminutive
6. effective
7. exclusive
8. native
9. negative
10. positive
11. primitive
12. productive
13. progressive
14. superlative
15. tentative

2-16 BUSCAPALABRAS: MYSTERY WORD!

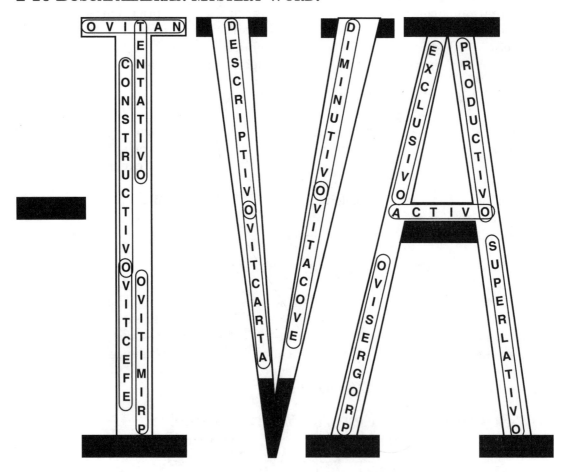

activo
atractivo
constructivo
descriptivo
diminutivo
efectivo
exclusivo

nativo
primitivo
progresivo
productivo
superlativo
tentativo
EVOCATIVO—not on list

2-17 MORE COGNATES: ENGLISH FOR SPANISH

1. cablegram
2. program
3. theorem (equation, formula)
4. problem
5. emblem
6. monogram
7. poem
8. telegram

2-18 SPANISH FOR ENGLISH

1. documento
2. elemento
3. impedimento
4. incremento
5. ligamento
6. movimiento
7. sacramento
8. sedimento
9. sentimiento
10. temperamento

2-19 SPANISH "-OSO/A" TO ENGLISH "-OUS"

1. ambicioso (a)
2. calamitoso (a)
3. caprichoso (a)
4. curioso (a)
5. delicioso (a)
6. fabuloso (a)
7. famoso (a)
8. generoso (a)
9. impetuoso (a)
10. industrioso (a)
11. malicioso (a)
12. religioso (a)
13. victorioso (a)

14. f a m oso (a)   (famous)
15. c u r i oso (a)   (curious)
16. g e n e r oso (a)   (generous)
17. r e l i g i oso (a)   (religious)
18. v i c t o r i oso (a)   (victorious)
19. i n d u s t r i oso (a)   (industrious)

2-20 "-OUS" IN ACTION

1. El gladiador victorioso comió una porción abundante de la deliciosa comida preparada especialmente para esta fabulosa ocasión por el cocinero del rey.
2. El estudiante ambicioso saca notas fabulosas.
3. George Washington, el famoso héroe de la revolución americana, fue también el primer presidente de los Estados Unidos.
4. La Madre Teresa es una persona generosa y religiosa.

2-21 "-IN" TO "-INA" OR "-INO"

1. aspirina
2. disciplina
3. gasolina
4. gelatina
5. medicina
6. parafina
7. sardina
8. vitamina
9. alpino
10. marino
11. femenino
12. pingüino

2-22 JUST ADD "-E"

1. accidente
2. competente
3. constante
4. continente
5. decente
6. diferente
7. elegante
8. evidente
9. excelente
10. importante
11. restaurante
12. tolerante
13. vigilante
14. penitente

2-23 ENGLISH "-ATE" VERBS TO SPANISH "-AR" VERBS

1. alienar
2. amputar
3. apreciar
4. coagular
5. comunicar
6. compensar
7. contaminar
8. debilitar
9. evaluar
10. indicar
11. implicar
12. operar
13. penetrar
14. recuperar
15. renovar
16. resucitar

2-24 FIGURE ME OUT!

ENGLISH
1. C   ontrol
2. O   riginal
3. G   eneral
4. N   ominal
5. A   ngel
6. T   error
7. E   clipse
8. S   uperior

SPANISH
1. control
2. original
3. general
4. nominal
5. ángel
6. terror
7. eclipse
8. superior

2-25 WATCH OUT! ¡FALSOS AMIGOS!

1. María está muy avergonzada.
2. La burla del payaso era chistosa.
3. Mis padres están de vacaciones.
4. El perro de Juan está sano ahora.
5. El criminal no estaba cuerdo.
6. El vagabundo cayó en una trampa.

2-26 MÁS FALSOS AMIGOS

1. arena
2. emocionante
3. simpático
4. red
5. pan
6. campo

Section 3: PARTS OF SPEECH

3-2 ¿CÓMO SE DICE EN ESPAÑOL?

1. Estoy empezando a comprender el problema.
2. Estamos aprendiendo español.
3. Los estudiantes están escribiendo la lección.
4. Yo he charlado con mis amigos.
5. Tú me has convencido.
6. Los obreros han seguido las instrucciones.
7. Yo había comprado el libro.
8. Tú habías obedecido a tus padres.
9. Nosotros habíamos dormido bien.

3-3 FIND ME!

1. <u>industrial:</u> adjetivo; modifica el nombre "nación."
2. <u>Jeréz, Málaga:</u> nombres propios, geográficos.
3. <u>forman:</u> verbo, activo.
4. <u>más:</u> adverbio; modifica el adjetivo "grande."
5. <u>El Cid:</u> nombre propio de una persona.
6. <u>ha cantado:</u> presente perfecto del verbo "cantar."
7. <u>de, la:</u> preposición; artículo definido.
8. <u>época:</u> nombre objetivo; objeto de la preposición "de."
9. <u>que:</u> pronombre relativo; se refiere al nombre "música."
10. <u>gente:</u> nombre colectivo.
11. <u>esto:</u> pronombre demostrativo.
12. <u>nosotros:</u> pronombre personal nominativo.
13. <u>lo:</u> pronombre objetivo; objeto del verbo "digo."
14. <u>estamos pensando:</u> presente progresivo del verbo "pensar."
15. <u>y:</u> conjunción; junta dos nombres.
16. <u>habían conquistado:</u> pluscuamperfecto del verbo "conquistar."
17. <u>estábamos comiendo:</u> pasado progresivo del verbo "comer."
18. Unscramble the circled letters: z o e a s p a m c b e r = rompecabezas (puzzle) (rompe cabezas, literally—head breaker)

3-4 NON-CONFORMISTS

1. la mano
2. el drama
3. el clima
4. el mapa
5. el programa
6. la foto
7. el planeta
8. el problema
9. la radio
10. el idioma
11. el telegrama
12. la moto

Section 4: SUSTANTIVOS

4-2 UNA FAMILIA CARIÑOSA (A LOVING FAMILY)

The López family—father, mother, son, daughter—are eating a meal that the mother has prepared with much care because it is her husband's birthday.

> **Mrs. López:** (to her husband) My dear, do you like the little meal I have prepared especially to please my beloved husband?
>
> **Mr. López:** Well, yes, darling (little wife), it's delicious; right, (little) Son, (little) Daughter?
>
> **Son:** Of course, (little) Father! Right, (little) Sister?
>
> **Daughter:** I should say so, (little) Brother! Thank you, (little) Mother!

Notice how the use of diminutives shows us that the members of this family love one another. Of course, in English it may sound exaggerated, but not so much in Spanish. The diminutives used are:

amorcito (amor)
comidita (comida)
maridito (marido)

papacito (papá)
hermanita (hermana)
hermanito (hermano)

mujercita (mujer) mamacita (mamá)
hijito (hijo) casita (casa)
hijita (hija)

4-3 ¿MASCULINO O FEMENINO?

```
A C C I D E N T E T A B M O C
U N A M I Z U R E D N E D R O
T O S R A I Z I M E T R E U S
O Z I A M L T B O R O R R E T
M A R C A L B U M A R R O Z U
O R I E N T E N E J A S N E M
V E G E T A L A P O E L I A B
I M A G E N I L O I V I G O R
L E N G U A J E S I S A F N E
T S O Z N C U V O Z E B U U T
E T I N E E G U A N T E R N R
T O S E M I U L D U A H O O O
N W I V I T E E D I M A R I P
A A V E R E T G Z L O S O V S
T E E I C Y E N I A T E T A N
S B L N O R T A P Ñ O M O B A
N U E L A M I N A E R U M O R
I N T E R E S O L S E R R O T
```

1. accident (el accidente)
2. airplane (el avión)
3. album (el album)
4. angel (el ángel)
5. animal (el animal)
6. automobile (el automóvil)
7. boss (el patrón)
8. cloud (la nube)
9. combat (el combate)
10. corn (el maíz)
11. cough (la tos)
12. crime (el crimen)
13. custom (la costumbre)
14. dance (el baile)
15. diamond (el diamante)
16. emphasis (el énfasis)
17. furor (el furor)
18. glove (el guante)
19. image (la imagen)
20. instant (el instante)
21. interest (el interés)
22. language (el lenguaje)
23. luck (la suerte)
24. message (el mensaje)
25. month (el mes)
26. motor (el motor)
27. name (el nombre)
28. net (la red)
29. noise (el rumor)
30. oil (el aceite)
31. order (el orden)
32. orient (el oriente)
33. pencil (el lápiz)
34. pyramid (la pirámide)
35. reason (la razón)
36. rice (el arroz)
37. root (la raíz)
38. sea (el mar)
39. sign (la señal)
40. snow (la nieve)
41. sun (el sol)
42. television (la televisión)
43. terror (el terror)
44. tomato (el tomate)
45. tower (la torre)
46. toy (el juguete)
47. transportation (el transporte)
48. tribunal (el tribunal)
49. vegetable (el vegetal)
50. vigor (el vigor)
51. violin (el violín)
52. voice (la voz)

4-4 TRES COSAS

uno	(1)	El accidente fue terrible.
tres	(3)	El acordeón no tiene cuerdas.
cinco	(5)	La actitud de Carlos es mala.
siete	(7)	La actriz es una estrella.
nueve	(9)	El alcohol no es bueno para la salud.
once	(11)	El algodón se usa para calcetines.
trece	(13)	El arroz se come con pollo.
quince	(15)	El balcón da al jardín.
diecisiete (diez y siete)*	(17)	El botón de la camisa es blanco.
diecinueve (diez y nueve)*	(19)	La calle es estrecha.
veintiuno (veinte y uno)*	(21)	La canción de los pájaros es agradable.
veintitrés (veinte y tres)*	(23)	El cheque es parte de la chequera.
veinticinco (veinte y cinco)*	(25)	La colección es muy completa.
veintisiete (veinte y siete)*	(27)	El crimen fue horrible.
veintinueve (veinte y nueve)*	(29)	El deporte es saludable.
treinta y uno	(31)	El detalle es importante.
treinta y tres	(33)	La edad del hombre no se sabía.
treinta y cinco	(35)	El examen fue muy difícil.
treinta y siete	(37)	La flor es amarilla.
treinta y nueve	(39)	La frente es parte de la cara.
cuarenta y uno	(41)	La frase es muy simple.
cuarenta y tres	(43)	La gente generalmente es buena.
cuarenta y cinco	(45)	La habitación
cuarenta y siete	(47)	El honor
cuarenta y nueve	(49)	El hotel
cincuenta y uno	(51)	El interés
cincuenta y tres	(53)	El jardín
cincuenta y cinco	(55)	El lápiz
cincuenta y siete	(57)	La libertad
cincuenta y nueve	(59)	El limón
sesenta y uno	(61)	El maíz
sesenta y tres	(63)	El mar
sesenta y cinco	(65)	El motor
sesenta y siete	(67)	La nación
sesenta y nueve	(69)	La nieve
setenta y uno	(71)	El origen
setenta y tres	(73)	La opinión
setenta y cinco	(75)	El país
setenta y siete	(77)	El pan
setenta y nueve	(79)	El papel
ochenta y uno	(81)	La parte
ochenta y tres	(83)	El plan
ochenta y cinco	(85)	La profesión
ochenta y siete	(87)	La protección
ochenta y nueve	(89)	La región
noventa y uno	(91)	La salud
noventa y tres	(93)	La sed
noventa y cinco	(95)	La tarde
noventa y siete	(97)	El tenis
noventa y nueve	(99)	El uniforme
ciento uno	(101)	La voz

*Two ways of spelling.

4-5 Números: Unas indicaciones más

1. 16 — diez y seis (dieciséis) alumnos
2. 101 — ciento una voces
3. 200 — doscientas mujeres
4. 1,000,000 — un millón de años
5. 21 — veinte y un (veintiún) lápices
6. 1996 — mil novecientos noventa y seis
7. $5.35 — cinco dólares (con) treinta y cinco (centavos)
8. 100 — cien películas
9. 102 — ciento dos estudiantes
10. 300 — trescientos soldados

4-6 Read the Star

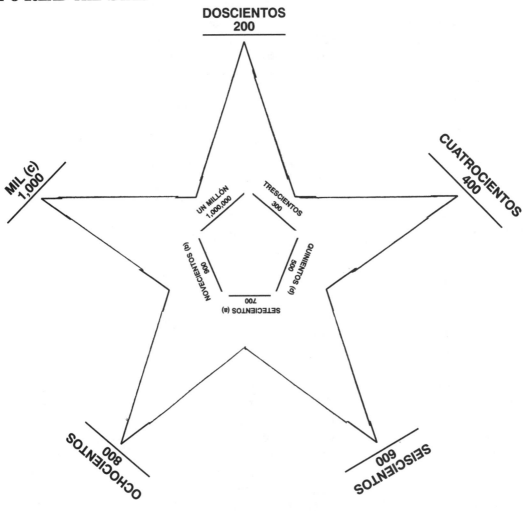

Estamos en el año <u>mil novecientos noventa y siete.</u>

Section 5: SINÓNIMOS

5-1 ¡Busque el sinónimo!

1. acabar	terminar	to end
2. andar	caminar	to walk
3. atravesar	cruzar	to cross

4. conducir	guiar	to drive
5. comprender	entender	to understand
6. contestar	responder	to answer
7. colocar	poner	to place
8. enviar	mandar	to send
9. reunir	juntar	to join together
10. suceder	ocurrir	to occur

WHAT ARE THEY?

t c c g e r p m j o	comer	coger	cocer
synonyms	cenar	tomar	guisar

THE RIGHT VERB

1. suceder
2. conducir
3. terminar

4. mandar
5. caminar, andar

5-2 MATCH ME WITH ANOTHER ADJECTIVE

1. aplicado	diligente	diligent
2. bastante	suficiente	sufficient, enough
3. célebre	famoso	famous
4. delgado	flaco	thin
5. grave	serio	serious
6. hábil	proficiente	proficient
7. indiferente	descuidado	indifferent
8. ingenioso	creativo	creative
9. navegable	dirigible	navigable
10. obstinado	tenaz	obstinate

5-3 DESCRIBE ME

1. hábil, proficiente
2. famoso, célebre
3. creativa, ingeniosa
4. flaco, delgado

5. obstinado, tenaz
6. célebre, famoso
7. navegable, dirigible

5-4 FIND MY NOUN MATE

1. la alcoba	el dormitorio	bedroom
2. el amo	el dueño	owner
3. el automóvil	el coche	car, auto
4. el cabello	el pelo	hair
5. la cárcel	la prisión	prison
6. el cura	el sacerdote	priest
7. la dama	la señora	lady
8. el edificio	el inmueble	building
9. el idioma	la lengua	language, tongue
10. el lugar	el sitio	place

MYSTERY NOUN

a a (a) c c c (d) (e) (i) l = idea

247

5-5 THE RIGHT NOUN, PLEASE

1. automóvil, coche
2. dama, señora
3. dormitorio - alcoba
4. amo, dueño
5. cárcel, prisión - lugar, sitio

5-6 SUSTANTIVOS OPUESTOS

1. el amigo	el enemigo	friend - enemy
2. el amor	el odio	love - hate
3. la dama	el caballero	lady - gentleman
4. el norte	el sur	north - south
5. la paz	la guerra	peace - war
6. la entrada	la salida	entrance - exit
7. el frío	el calor	cold - heat
8. el éxito	el fracaso	success - failure
9. la muerte	la vida	death - life
10. el verano	el invierno	summer - winter

5-7 MYSTERY NOUNS

1. éxito   fracaso
2. muerte   vida
3. invierno   frío; verano - calor
4. norte   sur
5. entrada   salida
6. amor   odio
7. guerra   paz
8. caballero   dama
9. amigo   enemigo
10. frío   calor

5-8 VERB ANTONYMS

1. abrir	cerrar	open - close
2. aparecer	desaparecer	appear - disappear
3. callar	hablar	keep quiet - speak
4. contestar	preguntar	answer - ask
5. encender	apagar	light - extinguish
6. jugar	trabajar	play - work
7. perder	ganar	lose - win
8. recordar	olvidar	remember - forget
9. salir	entrar	go out - come in
10. subir	bajar	go up - come down

5-10 ADJECTIVE ANTONYMS

1. alto	bajo	tall - short
2. ausente	presente	absent - present
3. blando	duro	soft - hard
4. bueno	malo	good - bad
5. corto	largo	short - long
6. difícil	fácil	difficult - easy
7. grande	pequeño	large - small
8. mejor	peor	better - worse
9. mismo	diferente	same - different
10. obscuro	claro	dark - light

Section 6: PREFIXES AND SUFFIXES

6-2 COMPLETE THE WORDS

1. condominio
2. predecir
3. telescopio
4. ilegal
5. anfiteatros
6. anteayer
7. dislocó
8. anormal
9. colaboran
10. prefijo
11. intransitable (impassable)
12. microscopio
13. profeta; pronosticar (predict)
14. superable (surmountable)
15. telescopio (telescope)

6-3 LOOK-ALIKES BUT DIFFERENT

1. ante-   (before) antepagar (prepay)
2. anti-   (in opposition) anticuerpo (antibody)
3. con-   (together) convivir (live together)
4. contra- (against) contracorriente (crosscurrent)
5. inter-   (between) intercambio (interchange)
6. intra-   (inside) intramuros (intramural; within the walls)
7. macro- (large) macroscópico (macroscopic; visible to the naked eye)
8. micro-   (small) microcosmo (microcosm; a little world)
9. pre-   (beforehand) precalentar (pre-heat)
10. pro-   (before) pronosticar (predict; prognosticate)
11. hiper-   (excess) hipertensión (hypertension)
12. hipo-   (under) hipodérmico (hypodermic; under the skin)

Section 7: PITFALLS

7-2 ¿DÓNDE ESTÁ?

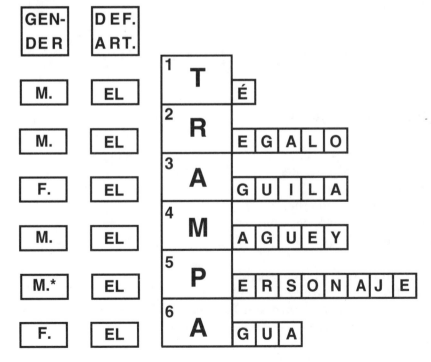

GEN-DER	DEF. ART.	
M.	EL	1 T É
M.	EL	2 R E G A L O
F.	EL	3 A GUILA
M.	EL	4 M AGUEY
M.*	EL	5 P ERSONAJE
F.	EL	6 A GUA

* The word itself is masculine, but it can refer to a feminine personage.

249

7-3 ¡COMPLÉTEME!

1. una pierna de hierro
2. de él
3. El águila; un ave de rapiña
4. mi
5. sólo
6. aparece; sólo; por la noche

7. En el campo
8. Voy a volver
9. personajes
10. pedir
11. dar un paseo
12. sabe

3. El águila
6. aparece
7. en el campo

5. sólo
6. por la noche

El águila aparece en el campo sólo por la noche.
(The eagle appears in the country only at night.)

7-5 ¿CÓMO SE DICE?

Miguel: ¿Qué tal, Carlos?

Carlos: Pues, nada en particular. Me siento un poco cansado.

Miguel: ¿Cansado? ¿Por qué?

Carlos: Pues, anoche a eso de las once me acosté. Estaba leyendo "El Cid Campeador" en cama, cuando alguien tocó a la puerta. ¡Qué raro! pensé. ¿Quién será a esta hora? En voz alta pregunté, "¿Quién es?" "Soy yo, Alberto," respondió la voz. Me di cuenta de que era mi nuevo vecino. En la oscuridad no vio el número de la puerta y se había equivocado. Me pidió perdón y se fue. Yo seguí leyendo "El Cid," y luego me quedé dormido boca arriba y soñé con mi héroe, el Campeador, siguiéndole a caballo toda la noche.

Section 8: REFRANES

8-3 REFRANES DE SABIDURÍA

1. Practice makes perfect.
2. The sun shines on all alike.
3. Better late than never.
4. One hand washes the other.
5. He who does not work does not eat.
6. Look before you leap.
7. Live and let live.
8. Not everything that shines is gold.
9. Don't rest on your laurels.
10. Tell me who your friends are and I'll tell you who you are.
11. Curiosity killed the cat.
12. After the rain comes the sun.

© 1996 by the Center for Applied Research in Education

© 1996 by the Center for Applied Research in Education

8-4 ¡Busque usted mi otra parte!

1. (6) En boca cerrada no entran moscas.
   (No flies enter a closed mouth.)
2. (3) Los pájaros de la misma pluma vuelan juntos.
   (Birds of a feather flock together.)
3. (4) No dejes para mañana lo que puedes hacer hoy.
   (Don't leave for tomorrow what you can do today.)
4. (8) A quien madruga Dios le ayuda.
   (The early bird catches the worm.)
5. (10) Más vale pájaro en mano que cien volando.
   (A bird in the hand is worth more than two in the bush.)
6. (7) Perro que ladra no muerde.
   (A barking dog does not bite.)
7. (2) Quien siembra vientos recoje tempestades.
   (You reap what you sow.)
8. (1) Ojos que no ven, corazón que no siente.
   (Out of sight, out of mind.)
9. (5) A caballo regalado no se le mira el colmillo.
   (Don't look a gift horse in the mouth.)
10. (9) A buen entendedor pocas palabras.
    (A word to the wise is sufficient.)
11. (11) ¡Haz lo que digo; no hagas lo que hago!
    (Do as I say; don't do as I do.)

Section 9: ALIMENTOS

9-2 "Cierto" es más fácil que "falso"

1. Falso. Según María, el amor entra por la cocina.
2. Cierto.
3. Falso. El plato favorito del novio de María es arroz con pollo.
4. Cierto.
5. Falso. María cuenta las calorías.
6. Falso. El hierro produce hemoglobina que lleva oxígeno a las células.
7. Cierto.
8. Falso. María y Roberto están de acuerdo en todo.
9. Falso. Cuando María y Roberto se casen, Roberto va a cocinar.
10. Falso. Para María y Roberto la salud es muy importante.
11. Falso. Alicia quiere lucir como las modelos de la televisión.

9-4 ¡Sea honesto/a!

Give an honest answer in Spanish to the following questions. Answers will vary.
1. Do you get along well with your brothers and sisters?
2. If not, why?
3. How many brothers and sisters do you have?
   Older? Younger?
4. Are your parents strict with you?
5. Are your parents fair with you?
6. Do you think that being parents is easy?
In class discuss family problems and ties (in Spanish as much as possible).

9-5 Es verdad

1. Obesity is a mental state which stems from boredom and sadness.
2. Tell me what you eat and I will tell you what you are.
3. There is no love more sincere than the love of food.

9-6 Consejo

COMMAND (UD.)	INFINITIVE
coma	comer
beba	beber
diviértase	divertirse

Eat, drink, and enjoy yourself,
Coma, beba y diviertase,

but tomorrow—
pero mañana—

DIET!
¡DIETA!

9-7 Out of One, Many

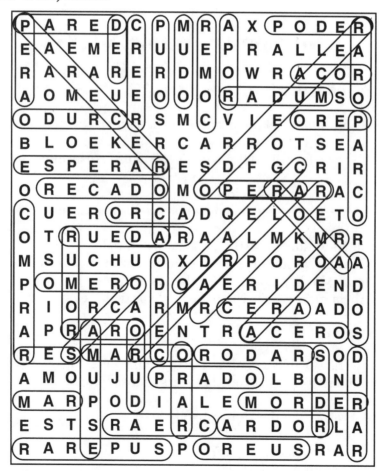

Note: 50 words from "Supermercado" are circled in the above square. The entire list of 95 follows.

95 WORDS FROM **SUPERMERCADO**

acero (steel, n.)
amo (master, n.)
amor (love, n.)
amado (beloved, adj.)
caer (to fall, v.)
campo (countryside, n.)
capa (cape, adj.)
cedro (cedar, n.)
cepo (vise, snare, n.)
cera (wax, n.)
cerdo (pig, n.)
come (he eats, v.)
comer (to eat, v.)
compra (a purchase, n.)
comprar (to purchase, v.)
copa (glass, goblet, n.)
creado (pp. of "crear")
crear (to create, v.)
credo (creed, n.)
creer (to believe, v.)
crema (cream, n.)
creo (I believe, v.)
crudo (raw, adj.)
cuera (leather jacket, n.)
cuerda (rope, n.)
cuerdo (sane, adj.)
cuero (pelt, n.)
dar (to give, v.)
doma (restraint, n.)
domar (to tame, v.)
dorar (to gild, v.)
dos (two, adj.)
durar (to last, v.)

duro (hard, adj.)
espera (an awaiting, n.)
ere ("r", n.)
esperar (to hope, wait, v.)
espero (I hope, v.)
espuma (foam, n.)
espumar (to skim, v.)
mar (sea, n.)
marco (frame, n.)
mero (mere, adj.)
moda (fashion, n.)
morder (to bite, v.)
mudar (to move, v.)
mudo (mute, adj.)
ópera (opera, n.)
operar (to operate, v.)
orar (to pray, v.)
orca (killer whale, n.)
padecer (to suffer, v.)
parco (frugal, adj.)
pardo (drab, adj.)
parecer (to appear, v.)
pared (wall, n.)
pecado (sin, n.)
perder (to lose, v.)
pero (but, conj.)
pera (pear, n.)
par (pair, n.)
poder (to be able, v. power, n.)
pomar (apple orchard, n.)
por (for, prep.)
prado (meadow, n.)

pues (well, therefore, conj.)
puma (puma, n.)
puro (pure, adj.)
raer (to scrape, v.)
ramo (branch, n.)
raro (strange, adj.)
recado (message, n.)
recuerdo (memory, n. I remember, v.)
red (net, n.)
remar (to row, v.)
remo (oar, n.)
res (cattle, n.)
resumo (I summarize, v.)
resecar (to dry up, v.)
roca (rock, n.)
rodar (to shoot a film, v.)
romper (to break, v.)
ropa (clothing, n.)
rueda (wheel, n.)
ruedo (rotation, n.)
rumor (noise, n.)
saco (sack, n.)
sapo (toad, n.)
sardo (Sardinian, n., adj.)
ser (to be, n.)
soda (soda, n.)
sudor (perspiration, n.)
suero (serum, whey, n.)
sumo (extreme, adj.)
superar (to overcome, v.)

50 WORDS FROM **SUPERMERCADO** WITHIN THE LETTER SQUARE

acero	dos	parco	remar
ardor	durar	parecer	remo
amor	duro	pared	res
cerdo	esperar	pera	roca
cera	espuma	pero	rodar
comer	mar	poder	romper
comprar	marco	prado	ropa
creado	morder	puro	rueda
crear	mudar	raro	rumor
creer	mudo	recado	saco
crudo	operar	recuerdo	soda
dar	orar	red	suero
	orca		superar

(contractions: pp = past participle; adj. = adjective; conj. = conjunction; n. = noun; v. = verb)

253

9-11 COLORES

1. las fresas, las manzanas
2. los limones, las toronjas, el durazno, la banana
3. uvas (f.) y ciruelas (f.)
4. las pasas, los higos, los dátiles
5. aguacates (m.) y peras (f.)
6. sandía (f.)
7. el aguacate
8. piña (f.)
9. el durazno, la banana

9-12 FIND THE MEAT AND POULTRY

CARNE (MEAT)

1	el biftec (steak)
2	la carne de cerdo (pork)
3	la carne de cordero (lamb)
9	la carne de res (beef)
4	la carne de ternera (veal)
11	el chorizo (also, la salchicha)
8	la hamburguesa (hamburger)
10	el hígado (liver)
5	el jamón (ham)
7	el perro caliente (hot dog)
6	el tocino (bacon)

FIND THE MEAT

Find the meat terms in English—diagonally, vertically, horizontally, and backwards. Circle each item; the first letter is numbered. Write that number in front of its Spanish counterpart on the list.

AVES CASERAS (POULTRY)

4	la gallina (hen)
3	el pato (duck)
1	el pavo (turkey)
2	el pollo (chicken)

FIND THE POULTRY

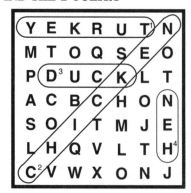

PESCADO (FISH)

- ✓ la almeja (clam)
- la anchoa (anchovy)
- el arenque (herring)
- el atún (tuna)
- el bacalao (codfish)
- el calamar (squid)
- ✓ el camarón (shrimp)
- ✓ el cangrejo (crab)
- ✓ el caracol (snail)
- ✓ la langosta (lobster)
- el lenguado (flounder; sole)
- ✓ el mejillón (mussel)
- la merluza (hake)
- ✓ la ostra (oyster)
- el pulpo (octopus)
- el salmón (salmon)
- la sardina (sardine)
- la trucha (trout)

9-13 SHELL ME

Circle the shellfish and check them off on the list.

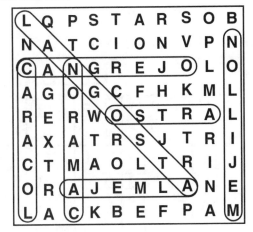

9-15 AHORA, LE TOCA A USTED

BUSCAPALABRAS

aceituna	caracol	guisante	melón	rábano
ajo	cebolla	habichuela	mole	res
albaricoque	cerdo	hamburguesa	naranja	salsa
alcachofa	coliflor	langosta	palomita de	salmón
almeja	cordero	lechuga	maíz	toronja
apio	escarola	lenteja	patata	trucha
atún	frambuesa	limón	pavo	taco
bacalao	fresa	mango	perejil	ternera
batido	galleta	mantequilla	pimiento	tomate
calamar	gallina	mariscos	piña	uva
camote	garbanzo	mayonesa	plátano	zanahoria
cangrejo	guacamole	manzana	pulpo	

9-16 ¿Lo sabe usted ?

1. manzana
2. Manzana de la Discordia
3. la fruta (la manzana) del Árbol de Sabiduría
   (The Tree of Knowledge)

9-17 Más alimentos

BUSCAPALABRAS

G	U	A	R	E	N	R	E	T	A	I	R	A	M	E	J	I	L	L	O	N
O	A	O	H	C	N	A	X	O	L	S	A	L	P	O	Z	I	R	O	H	C
V	T	L	A	U	X	L	A	C	A	R	A	C	O	L	O	J	A	A	A	R
E	S	A	L	M	O	N	M	I	M	A	D	R	E	T	I	O	Z	U	M	O
S	A	R	P	I	S	P	E	N	A	L	O	A	L	E	G	U	A	R	B	A
E	R	M	I	N	N	A	N	O	R	E	S	C	O	L	L	A	R	A	U	B
R	D	A	R	T	I	A	R	E	N	Q	U	E	T	R	U	D	E	A	R	E
O	I	R	P	E	T	Y	A	A	K	U	S	R	E	O	V	I	D	A	G	S
A	N	O	A	R	S	O	C	S	I	R	A	M	Y	D	A	O	N	O	U	T
M	A	J	U	S	T	A	O	R	A	R	L	A	M	E	R	D	O	D	E	S
K	I	E	L	O	A	T	S	O	P	A	Y	N	H	O	B	A	R	A	S	W
A	T	R	O	P	R	A	F	C	T	H	R	A	L	C	O	G	A	U	A	D
A	M	G	S	L	T	H	O	S	R	I	A	N	T	O	I	I	M	G	R	C
J	A	N	C	U	W	R	O	I	U	D	M	A	O	L	N	H	A	N	F	E
E	L	A	N	P	D	G	Z	O	C	R	A	B	S	M	O	O	C	E	N	R
M	O	C	I	E	N	T	I	G	H	O	L	A	T	O	M	N	V	L	I	D
L	S	B	R	A	S	I	L	E	A	N	A	I	R	B	A	C	A	L	A	O
A	S	O	L	I	T	A	R	A	S	O	C	R	A	N	J	U	M	P	N	S

el ajo	la col	la res
la almeja	el cordero	la sal
la anchoa	la gallina	la salchicha
el arenque	la hamburguesa	el salmón
el atún	el hígado	la sardina
el bacalao	el jamón	la sopa
la banana	la langosta	el té
el calamar	el lenguado	la ternera
el camarón	el mejillón	el tocino
el cangrejo	la merluza	la trucha
el caracol	la ostra	la uva
la carne	el pan	el zumo
el cerdo	el pato	
el chorizo	el pulpo	

© 1996 by the Center for Applied Research in Education

9-18 LA PAELLA VALENCIANA

Algunos ingredientes:
el ajo (garlic)
la almeja (clam)
el arroz (rice)
el camarón (shrimp)
el cangrejo (crab)

la cebolla (onion)
el mejillón (mussel)
el pollo (chicken)
el tomate (tomato)
el limón
sal y pimienta (salt and pepper)

9-19 ¡PONGA LA MESA PARA EL DESAYUNO! (SET THE TABLE FOR BREAKFAST.)

Alimentos que se pueden servir para el desayuno. (Food items that may be served for breakfast.)
el jugo de naranja (orange juice)
el jugo de toronja (grapefruit juice)
la leche (milk)
el café (coffee)
la mantequilla (butter)
los huevos (eggs)
la mermelada (jam, marmalade)

el pastelito (tart)
la miel (honey)
el tocino (bacon)
el pan tostado (toast)
el panecillo (roll)
el té (tea)
la sal y la pimienta (salt and pepper)

¡Buen provecho! (Hearty appetite!)

9-20 ¡ARRÉGLEME!

1. Los niños tienen que beber leche cada día.
   (Children have to drink milk every day.)
2. Popeye tiene músculos porque come espinacas cada día.
   (Popeye has muscles because he eats spinach every day.)
3. El limón no es dulce, sino agrio.
   (The lemon is not sweet, but sour.)
4. Cortar una cebolla cruda es muy triste porque me hace llorar.
   (Cutting a raw onion is very sad because it makes me cry.)
5. Me gustan los macarrones con salsa, y también me gusta la música llamada "salsa."
   (I like macaroni with sauce, and I also like the music called "salsa.")
6. La interesante ciudad de Boston es famosa por sus frijoles.
   (The interesting city of Boston is famous for its beans.)
7. El color de los pepinos no es rojo.
   (The color of cucumbers is not red.)
8. Las zanahorias no crecen en los árboles.
   (Carrots do not grow on trees.)
9. Dicen que si comes mucho pescado, vas a ser muy inteligente.
   (They say that if you eat a lot of fish, you will be very intelligent.)
10. En "McDonald's" sirven hamburguesas, patatas fritas y otros platos ricos.
    (At McDonald's they serve hamburgers, French fries, and other delicious dishes.)

p e t m i o i n s
(P I M I E N T O S)

LISTA

la leche	los frijoles
las espinacas	los pepinos
el limón	las zanahorias
la cebolla	el pescado
la salsa	las patatas fritas
los macarrones	las hamburguesas

9-21 ¿PERDER, GANAR O MANTENER?

Quiero perder peso. Para mi desayuno voy a comer.
> jugo de toronja (grapefruit juice)
> pan tostado (toast)
> un vaso de leche (glass of milk)
> café sin azúcar ni crema

Quiero ganar peso. Para mi desayuno voy a comer.
> jugo de naranja (orange juice)
> dos huevos revueltos con tocino (2 scrambled eggs, with bacon)
> panecillo con mantequilla y miel (roll with butter and honey)
> una banana
> un vaso de leche
> café con crema y azúcar

Quiero mantener el peso. Para mi desayuno voy a comer.
> jugo de naranja
> pan tostado con mermelada
> un vaso de leche con pastelitos

9-22 A ALGUNOS LES GUSTA NADAR

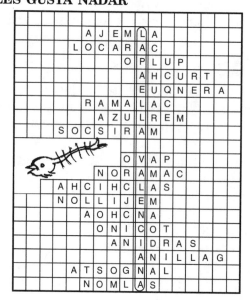

la almeja (clam)	el mejillón (mussel)
la anchoa (anchovy)	la merluza (hake)
el arenque (herring)	el pavo (turkey)
el calamar (squid)	el pulpo (octopus)
el caracol (snail)	la salchicha (sausage)
el camarón (shrimp)	el salmón (salmon)
la gallina (chicken)	la sardina (sardine)
la langosta (lobster)	el tocino (bacon)
los mariscos (shellfish)	la trucha (trout)

la paella valenciana

258

© 1996 by the Center for Applied Research in Education

9-23 No pertenece

1. mantequilla	No es vegetal.
2. limón	No es dulce.
3. carne	No es fruta.
4. manzana	No es seca.
5. cereza	No tiene corteza.
6. arenque	No es elemento nutritivo.
7. apio	No contiene almidón (starch).
8. piña	No es vegetal.
9. agua	No es producto de vaca (cow).
10. sal	No está hecha de harina (flour).
11. coliflor	No es carne.
12. albaricoque	No es fruta cítrica.
13. pavo	No es pescado.
14. tomate	No es ave.
15. trucha	No es marisco.

9-24 ¡Fiesta!

1. We give gifts.
2. We sing songs.
3. We dance.
4. We play (tocar) the piano.
5. We eat crackers with hot sauce.
6. We eat candy.
7. We eat potato chips.
8. We eat fruit: pears, bananas, apples, grapes.
9. We eat hot dogs.
10. We eat popcorn.
11. We eat ice cream.
    Las letras con círculos son: d i e c i s e i s.
    La persona festejada tiene d i e c i s é i s años.

9-25 ¿Qué se compra?

En la carnicería se compra carne.
En la cafetería se toma café y otras bebidas.
En la frutería se compran frutas.
En la heladería se venden helados.
En la lechería se compra leche y crema.
En la panadería se hace o se vende pan.
En la pastelería se hacen y se venden pasteles.
El supermercado es una tienda donde el cliente se sirve a sí mismo. Venden todo
    género de artículos alimenticios y otras cosas.

9-26 ¿Qué vas a preparar?

Tu mejor amigo quiere preparar una comida típicamente norteamericana para
un grupo de amigos hispanos.
    FREE REIN! Make up your favorite menus.
    Your Hispanic friends can prepare a menu typically Spanish, in
        return.

Section 10: HOGAR Y FAMILIA

10-1 Conozca usted a la familia hispana: (traducción)

In Hispanic society, family honor is very important. The young people are the pride of their relatives. It is their duty to uphold the family honor.

Family reunions are frequent. Holidays are celebrated with lavish dinners. Parents and their children spend time together in the country, at the beach, in theaters and in museums, thus maintaining family unity. Also, a good friend of the children is a friend of the entire family.

10-2 ¿Quién es?

1. hermano
2. prima
3. primos
4. sobrino
5. abuelo
6. bisabuelo
7. madrastra
8. hermanastra
9. cuñado
10. suegros
11. sobrina
12. bisnietos
13. resobrina
14. nietos

10-4 La familia González

1. Hay cuatro personas en la familia González.
2. La familia González está desayunándose.
3. No, hace buen tiempo.
4. El Sr. González propone ir de merienda al campo.
5. Sí, todos están de acuerdo.
6. La Sra. González y su hija, María, van a preparar la merienda.
7. Mientras tanto, el Sr. González y Carlos van a revisar el coche.
8. El Sr. González y Carlos tienen que comprar vasos y servilletas de papel, palomitas de maíz, hojuelas de patatas fritas y pan.
9. Antes de irse, el Sr. González les dice a su mujer y a María que no se olviden de preparar algo para las hormigas.
10. (Esta respuesta puede variar.)

10-5 Ir de camping (translation)

It is a long weekend, and the González family—mother, father, and children, Carlos and María—are going to go camping. In preparation, they are gathering together the necessary articles. In addition to clothing and food that Mrs. González and María are preparing, this camping trip must include:

tent	cooking pan
sleeping bag	flashlight
knapsack	binoculars
blanket	

After a good deal of excitment, everything is ready, and at dawn tomorrow they will start out.

10-6 ¡Olé!

la canasta de comestibles
¡Chévere!
la despensa
las hormigas
ir de merienda
la lechuga

las manzanas
revisar
las palomitas de maíz
las patatas fritas
la tortilla
las zanahorias

10-7 ¿Para qué sirve?

1. ir de camping
2. cargar las necesidades
3. mantenerse cómoda; dormir

4. cocinar; calentar la comida
5. ver cuando se hace de noche
6. ver a larga distancia

10-8 Más utensilios

un despertador
un botiquín
gafas negras para el sol
jabón y toallas
una bolsa de herramientas
    (martillo, sierra, clavos)

an alarm clock
a first-aid kit
sunglasses
soap and towels
a tool kit (hammer, saw, nails)

Note: There may be many others.

10-9 Cuartos, mueblas y componentes de una casa (Rooms, Furniture, and Home Components)

Generally, a room consists of four walls, a ceiling, a floor, some windows, and a door.

On the entrance door there is a security chain, a peephole, and the mail chute.

In the bedroom there is a bed with a mattress, pillows, a blanket, a bedspread, a chair, an armchair, a night table, and a lamp. There are curtains covering the window. On the night table there is an alarm clock. There is also a chest of drawers, a dressing table, and a clothes closet with a mirror.

In the family room there is a sofa, several arm chairs, a desk, some shelves for books or knicknacks, a TV set, a stereo, lamps, and pictures.

In the dining room there is a table with a tablecloth, several chairs, and a sideboard.

In the kitchen there are cupboards, a vacuum cleaner, a broom, a refrigerator, a washing machine, a dishwasher, a dryer, a freezer, a stove, and a fan. Other electrical appliances: a blender, a toaster, a can opener, a radio.

In the bathroom there is a bathtub, a shower, some bathroom fittings, bath towels, washcloths, a bath mat, and tiles. Other articles: bath slippers, bath soap, bath powder, bathrobe, shower cap.

In a private home there is a stairway that leads to the basement, a garage for the car and garden tools, and a garden.

10-10 Díme...

1. cuatro paredes
2. las paredes tienen oídos
3. mirilla; puerta de entrada
4. cama; colchón; almohadas; frazada; cubrecama
5. despertador; mesita de noche
6. butaca; sala de estar
7. comedor
8. refrigerador; cocina
9. lavadora de ropa
10. aparatos eléctricos
11. bañera; ducha; cuarto de baño
12. casa particular; sótano; garaje

10-11 ¿Cierto o falso?

1. Falso. La señora Fernández está cocinando.
2. Falso. Silvia está poniendo la mesa.
3. Falso. El señor Fernández está leyendo el periódico.
4. Cierto.
5. Falso. Manolo se queja frecuentemente

No debo...

Manolo no debe quejarse.
Silvia no debe criticar.

© 1996 by the Center for Applied Research in Education

10-12 ¿Dónde está mi lugar? (Where Is My Place?)

1. I put my clothes in <u>ropero</u> (closet).
2. María prepares the dinner in <u>cocina</u> (kitchen).
3. For dining, we take our seats at the table in <u>comedor</u> (dining room).
4. The children wash their hands in <u>cuarto de baño</u> (bathroom).
5. After dinner we have coffee in <u>sala de estar</u> (family room).
6. The visitors like to see the flowers in <u>jardín</u> (garden).
7. My father keeps wine bottles in <u>sótano</u> (basement).
8. My car is in <u>garaje</u> (garage).
9. Our visitors sleep in <u>dormitorio</u> (bedroom).
10. My mother cleans the rugs with <u>aspiradora</u> (vacuum cleaner).
11. In the living room I sit on <u>sofá</u> (sofa).
12. The curtains cover <u>ventanas</u> (windows).
13. My father shaves, looking in <u>espejo</u> (mirror).
14. The pictures are placed on <u>paredes</u> (walls).
15. The child sits in a small <u>silla</u> (chair).

10-13 ¡Búsqueme!

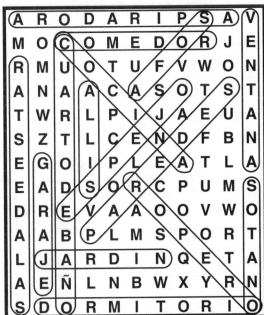

1. el ropero	9. el dormitorio
2. la cocina	10. la aspiradora
3. el comedor	11. el sofá
4. el cuarto de baño	12. las ventanas
5. la sala de estar	13. el espejo
6. el jardín	14. las paredes
7. el sótano	15. la silla
8. el garaje	

10-15 Translation: El primer día del semestre (The First Day of the Semester)

Manuel and his friend, Alberto, are walking to school.

Manuel: Are you happy going back to school?

Alberto: Well, yes and no. I prefer being on vacation.

Manuel: Yes, me too. How did you spend your vacation?

Alberto: Great! I spent several weeks with my cousin who lives in the country. We enjoyed ourselves walking through the woods, swimming in the pool, and playing tennis. Also, my aunt is a good cook.

Manuel: Well, lucky you. We stayed in the city. I think we're going to get our schedules for the new semester today.

Alberto: Could be. Did you get good grades last semester?

Manuel: More or less, but I didn't do too well in chemistry.

Alberto: In my case, history gave me problems. I'm going to stop playing soccer so that I can concentrate on my studies.

Manuel: Really? Well, here we are! See you later. Wait for me at dismissal.

Alberto: Okay. See you later!

10-16 School and Study (Translation)

In Hispanic countries school discipline is more rigorous than in the United States. A student is punished if he arrives late for class and if he does not do his homework. There are various punishments, including spending Saturday in school.

10-17 Rompecabezas: Palabras escolásticas

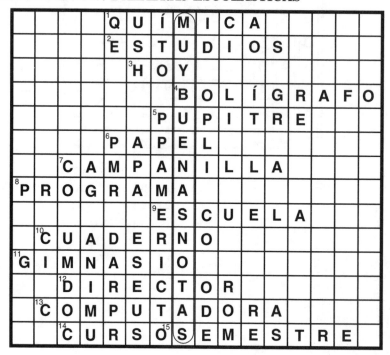

Palabras escolásticas: <u>Muy buenas notas</u> (very good grades)

© 1996 by the Center for Applied Research in Education

Section 11: VIAJAR (TRAVEL)

11-2 ¡COMPLÉTEME!

1. El despegue
2. boleto aéreo
3. objetos perdidos
4. aeropuerto, libre de aduana
5. equipaje, carreta

6. La azafata
7. El auxiliar de vuelo
8. coche cama
9. pasar por la aduana

11-3 ¡IDENTIFÍQUEME!

Tampico
Yucatán
Veracruz
Acapulco
Guadalajara

México
Chichen Itzá
Taxco
Mérida

11-4 STOPPING PLACES IN SPANISH-SPEAKING COUNTRIES

1. camarero; propina
2. botones; botones
3. mozo

4. dependiente
5. hostería

11-5 DIÁLOGO: EN EL HOTEL (IN THE HOTEL)

Traduzca:

Receptionist:	Good day. May I help you?
Mr. López	I'd like a single room.
Receptionist:	On what floor would you like it, and for how long?
Mr. López:	For three days. I prefer the top floor, with a view of the street. Could you show me one?
Receptionist:	Of course! With pleasure. We'll use the elevator.
Mr. López:	Are the rooms well ventilated?
Receptionist:	Yes, yes, and quiet too. (The receptionist shows him a room. Mr. López looks it over.)
Mr. López:	That's fine. It seems comfortable. I'll take this one.
Receptionist:	Good. Then let's go down and I'll give you the key; you'll do me the favor of signing the register. If you need anything, please press the buzzer.
Mr. López:	Thank you very much. For the moment I don't need anything more. I'm going to rest awhile.

11-6 CRUCIGRAMA

EPEAITOICRNSC (circled letters)
RECEPCIONISTA (hotel employee)

© 1996 by the Center for Applied Research in Education

Section 12: AUTOMOBILES

12-1 Dé usted las respuestas

1. Juan y Luis están en San José, la capital de Costa Rica.
2. Quieren alquilar un coche para ver los alrededores de la ciudad.
3. El coche que escogieron es verde.
4. No, las llantas tienen bastante aire.
5. No, el tanque de gasolina está lleno.
6. No, el radiador está lleno de agua.
7. Necesitan un coche con aire acondicionado porque hace calor.

12-2 Partes del Auto

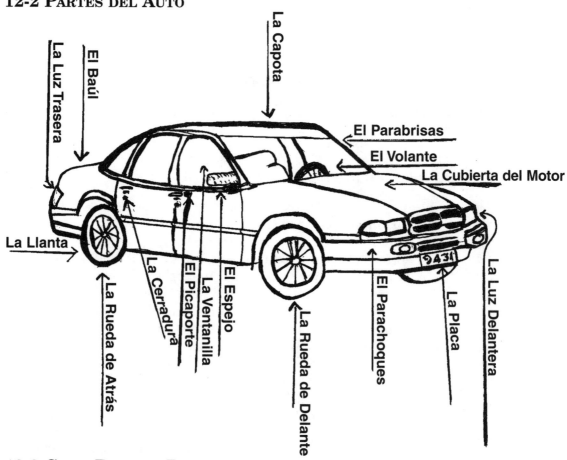

12-3 Good-Driving Rules

1. (2)
2. (4)
3. (7)
4. (10)
5. (11)

6. (6)
7. (5)
8. (8)
9. (9)
10. (3)
11. (1)

12-4 Herramientas útiles

1 llave de tuercas (la)
2 destornillador (el)
3 llave de tuercas simple (la)

4 martillo (el)
5 alicates (los)

© 1996 by the Center for Applied Research in Education

Section 13: DINING IN A RESTAURANT

13-3 ¡No lo podemos creer!

1. qué hay de comer
2. un cocido con las sobras de la semana.
3. tiene mucha hambre y que no le apetece un cocido.
4. restaurante "Buen Provecho."
5. un bistec con papas fritas y una ensalada de verduras.
6. no hay ni bistec, ni pollo, ni pescado, ni carne.
7. enojado.
8. tarde para el almuerzo.
9. hay una especialidad del día.
10. "Está bien, ¡tráiganosla!"
11. Les trae dos platos de cocido.
12. ¿Cree usted que el señor Gómez le debe dejar una propina (tip) al camarero?
    Sí, porque no era culpa del camarero.
    No, porque el camarero no les dio buen servicio.
    (¿Qué opinan ustedes?)
    ¡Discútanlo!

13-4 La palabra apropiada

1. postre
2. menú
3. bebida
4. un camarero, una camarera
5. tarde
6. Valencia
7. pescado
8. almuerzo
9. aperitivo
10. propina
11. nueve hasta las once de la noche
12. café, té o chocolate y pan dulce

13-5 Trabalenguas (Tongue Twister)

El autobús tiene cuatro <u>ruedas.</u>
(The bus has four wheels.)

Section 14: IR DE COMPRAS

14-1 Se equivocó

1. No, no lo es.
2. Él cree que no vale la pena saberlas porque su esposa, de todos modos, va a cambiar el regalo.
3. La empleada se comporta bien, con mucha paciencia.
4. Ella dudaba de que su esposo se recordara de su cumpleaños. También se sorprendió porque los guantes eran tan bonitos y de la medida exacta.
5. No, no es un mal hombre. Quiere hacer lo que hay que hacer. (He wants to do the right thing.)

14-2 LAS TIENDAS (¡COMPLÉTEME!)

1. cheques de viajero
2. demasiado caros
3. más baratos
4. escaparate
5. camisas
6. guantes
7. paraguas
8. escalera mecánica
9. caja
10. medidas
11. tiendas; nueve

14-4 MYSTERY WORD(S)

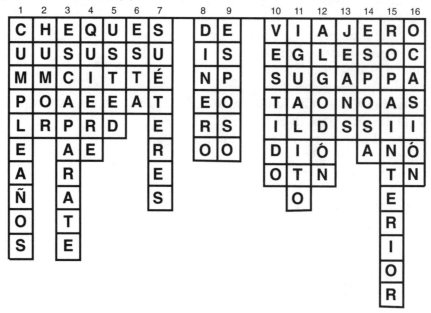

Mystery words (along the top row): CHEQUES DE VIAJERO (Traveller's checks)

Section 15: CONSULTING A DENTIST

15-1 DIALOGUE: I HAVE A TOOTHACHE.

Carmen has a swollen cheek which is very painful. She goes to the office of her dentist, Dr. Sacamuelas.

Dr. S.: Hi, Carmencita. What do you have in your mouth, an apple?

Carmen: Don't make fun of me, Doctor. I have an unbearable pain.

Dr. S.: Sorry, I see that you are suffering. Sit here in this chair; open your mouth and let me see the bad teeth. (After examining her teeth ...)

Dr. S.: I have to take some x-rays to see what's at the bottom of those two teeth. (The dentist finds that the two molars have cavities on the inside.)

Dr. S.: I thought so! The two molars are in bad shape. I can save one but I have to extract the other one.

Carmen: Will it hurt a lot?

Dr. S.:	No, you'll feel a slight prick when I give you an injection of anesthesia in the gum.		

Dr. S.: No, you'll feel a slight prick when I give you an injection of anesthesia in the gum.
(Without Carmen's realizing it, the dentist has extracted the bad molar.)

Dr. S.: Here's the cause of your pain.

Carmen: But I didn't feel anything!

Dr. S.: Good. I'm going to give you these pills should you have pain later on. See me in three days and we'll save the other molar.

Carmen: Thank you, Doctor. I think I feel better.

15-2 ¡COMPLÉTEME!

1. una mala muela
2. su dentista
3. manzana; mejilla hinchada
4. sillón
5. examina las muelas
6. unos rayos X de las muelas
7. están picadas en el interior
8. una muela; extraer
9. la mala muela; dolor
10. pastillas; más tarde
11. tres días
12. culpable; siente mejor

15-4 SEE WHO RATES THE HIGHEST

1. Se llaman "dientes de juicio" porque crecen entre los 17 y 25 años, cuando empezamos a tener más prudencia y sabiduría.
   (They are called "wisdom teeth" because they grow in between the ages of 17 and 25, when we start to have more prudence and wisdom.)
2. Se llaman "caninos" porque son puntiagudos como los dientes de perros.
   (They are called "canines" because they are pointed like dogs' teeth.)
3. Los dientes de leche. Los dientes permanentes.
4. lengua
5. las encías
6. las caries; el cepillo de dientes; la pasta de dientes (pasta dentífrica)
7. consultorio (del dentista); sillón
8. sacar rayos X; una muela
9. extraer; inyección
10. mala muela; hinchazón en la mejilla

Section 16: CONSULTING A DOCTOR

16-1 PARTS OF THE BODY

Possible answers for 1-5:

arm	el brazo	lip	el labio
ear	la oreja	toe	el dedo (del pie)
eye	el ojo	rib	la costilla
leg	la pierna	gum	la encía
hip	la cadera		

Possible answers for 6-10:

ankle	el tobillo	shoulder	el hombro
knee	la rodilla	head	la cabeza
elbow	el codo	back	la espalda
foot	el pie		

16-3 Dialogue: Small Tonsils, Big Problems

Mr. Reyes has had a sore throat for more than a week. Finally, he decides to consult his doctor, Dr. Arias. The doctor is wearing a white medical gown, and a stethoscope around his neck.

Dr. A.: Good day, Mr. Reyes. I haven't seen you in a while. What's happening?

Mr. R.: Well, my throat is very sore and each day it becomes more difficult to swallow.

Dr. A.: Let me examine you. Open your mouth; say "ah." (The doctor examines the patient's throat, his ears; he sounds his chest; takes his temperature and blood pressure.) How long have you had this sore throat?

Mr. R.: More than a week. What's the matter with me, Doctor?

Dr. A.: Your tonsils are very inflamed; you have a slight congestion in your lungs, and you have fever. Do your joints hurt?

Mr. R.: Yes, that also bothers me. What must be done, Doctor?

Dr. A.: I'm going to prescribe an antibiotic to control the infection. Take one pill every four hours for one week; then I want to see you again. But the only solution is to remove your tonsils. If not, this problem will recur.

Mr. R.: Thank you, Doctor. About the operation—I'll think about it. For the moment my work will not make it possible.

Dr. A.: Until later then. I hope you'll feel better soon.

16-4 ¡Búsqueme y tradúzcame!

antibiotic	el antibiótico
auscultate	auscultar (v.)
congestion	la congestión
consult	consultar (v.)
doctor	el médico; el doctor
examine	examinar (v.)
fever	la fiebre
infection	la infección
lungs	los pulmones
mouth	la boca
pain	el dolor
problem	el problema
tablet	la pastilla
temperature	la temperatura
throat	la garganta
tonsils	las amígdalas

© 1996 by the Center for Applied Research in Education

16-6 ¡Complétame!

1. acidez
2. hemorragia
3. dolores agudos
4. coágulo de sangre
5. calambre
6. indigestión
7. bronquitis
8. catarro, gripe
9. reumatismo
10. ampollas
11. hinchazón
12. virus

16-8 Ouch!

1. la alergia — allergy
2. la tos — cough
3. el calambre — cramp
4. la gripe — flu
5. el baño — bath
6. la bronquitis — bronchitis
7. el desmayo — fainting spell
8. la acidez — acidity
9. el mareo — dizziness
10. la hinchazón — swelling
11. el reumatismo — rheumatism
12. el dolor — pain

Las letras con círculos son: a b c r a e m l
La palabra es: calambre

(Note: All answers are nouns.)

Section 17: DEPORTES

17-2 Identifique usted el deporte (Identify the Sport)

(Exercise is the vital principle of health.)
1. Figure skating—male, female
2. Tennis—tennis racquet
3. Tennis—net on the tennis court, between the players
4. Ice skating—ice skate
5. Horseback riding—girl on horseback
6. Bicycling—helmet
7. Bowling—bowling balls
8. Bowling—bowling alley

17-3 ¡Búsqueme—en español!

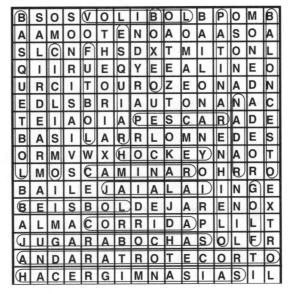

271

1. gymnastics	la corrida	15
2. volleyball	el jai alai	18
3. bicycling	la natación	16
4. golf	la gimnasia	1
5. bowling	el pescar	17
6. walking	el esquiar	14
7. basketball (2)	el béisbol	13
8. jogging	el patinar en hielo	11
9. soccer	el boxeo	12
10. hockey	el golf	4
11. ice skating	el ciclismo	3
12. boxing	el hockey	10
13. baseball	el vólibol	2
14. skiing	el fútbol	9
15. bullfighting	el baloncesto	7
16. swimming	jugar a las bochas	5
17. fishing	caminar	6
18. handball	andar a trote corto	8
	el básquetbol	7

17-4 ¡JUGUEMOS!

```
(1)  L P A T I N A R E N H I E L O
     W X O P L O S D E P O R T E S
(2)  N S T I A L A I A J R P Q U T
     S O N E J E R C I C I O S A M
(3)  A M B A L O N C E S T O C O N
     R U M B A A L F I S I C O S S
(4)  V E R D E F L O G A R P I S A
     A L I M E N T O S Q U E S O N
(5)  E F U T B O L V A M P I R E N
     S A L U D A B L E S Y C O N E
(6)  M E L E N A B E I S B O L O S
     A S A P A R A N I Ñ O S E L L
(7)  I S I N E T M A N O L O U N D
     Y N I N A S W A X I N G L O O
(8)  T R A E X O B M A N I O B R A
     V O C A C I O N H O M B R E S
(9)  C O M O E S X C I C L I S M O
     Y M U J E R E S B I L L E T O
(10) G L A M O L O B I L O V E N D
```

(1) ¡DÉME UN CÍRCULO!   (2) ¿QUÉ SE NECESITA?

1. Para patinar en hielo — se necesitan botas atadas a patines.
2. Para jugar al jai a-lai — se necesitan una pelota y un cesto atado al brazo.
3. Para jugar al baloncesto — se necesitan un balón y un cesto colocado a cierta altura.
4. Para jugar al golf — se necesitan una pelota de golf y varios palos.
5. Para jugar al fútbol — se necesitan una pelota y dos porterías.
6. Para jugar al béisbol — se necesitan una pelota, un bate y un guante especial.
7. Para jugar al tenis — se necesitan una pelota de tenis, una raqueta y una red que separa a los jugadores.
8. Para boxear — se necesitan un par de guantes especiales y un cuadrilátero.
9. Para el ciclismo — se necesitan una bicicleta y un casco para proteger la cabeza del ciclista.
10. Para jugar al vólibol — se necesitan un balón y una red que separa a los dos equipos.

(3) ¡DESCÍFREME!

Los deportes son ejercicios físicos que son saludables para niños y niñas, hombres y mujeres.

17-5 SPORTS (TRANSLATION)

There are many sports fans in the Hispanic countries. In addition to the general sports field, there are two sports that are typically Spanish—the bullfight and jai a-lai, a Basque sport similar to handball.

Every Sunday there are bullfights in Mexico and Spain. They are also popular in Peru and Colombia. The bullfight starts at four o'clock sharp. The parade of the bullfighters in the arena is an exciting spectacle. The "suit of lights" worn by the bullfighter is embroidered with silver and gold thread.

The parade consists of the following participants:

matador (kills the bull)
picador (a mounted bullfighter who wounds the bull with a pike)
capeador ("plays" the bull with a cape)

Sometimes one of the participants is gored by the bull.

The principal bullfighter manipulates a pole with a hanging cloth, generally red in color, with which he provokes the bull and forces him to lower his head when he is about to be killed.

There are two opposing forces here—the brutal strenght of an infuriated animal against the bravery and gracefulness of man.

The bullfighter is a national hero in both Spain and Mexico. In order to appreciate bullfighting we must understand the artistry and skill of the bullfighter.